FINANCIAL SECTOR OF THE AMERICAN ECONOMY

edited by
STUART BRUCHEY
ALLAN NEVINS PROFESSOR EMERITUS
COLUMBIA UNIVERSITY

A GARLAND SERIES

VALUATION OF CORPORATE GROWTH OPPORTUNITIES

A REAL OPTIONS APPROACH

Richard E. Ottoo

GARLAND PUBLISHING, INC.
A MEMBER OF THE TAYLOR & FRANCIS GROUP
NEW YORK & LONDON/2000

658.15
091~

Published in 2000 by
Garland Publishing, Inc.
A member of the Taylor & Francis Group
29 West 35th Street
New York, NY 10001

10 9 8 7 6 5 4 3 2 1

Library of Congress Cataloging-in-Publication Data

Ottoo, Richard E., 1958–
    Valuation of corporate growth opportunities : a real
options approach / Richard E. Ottoo.
        p. cm. — (Financial sector of the American
        economy)
    Includes bibliographical references and index.
    ISBN 0-8153-3783-3 (alk. paper)
        1. Corporations—Valuation. 2. Corporations—
Finance. 3. Options (Finance) I. Title. II. Series.

    HG4028.V3 O88 2000
    658.15—dc21
                                                    00-021544

Printed on acid-free, 250 year-life paper
Maufactured in the United States of America

To my daughter Emily, my greatest gift and source of happiness and in memory of my parents, Sabina and Jevenino, for their love, care and wisdom.

Preface

This book is my contribution to the global efforts underway to find solutions to critical corporate valuation challenges. Recent advances in real options pricing theories have revolutionized corporate investment decision-making. For instance, we are now capable of recommending that a negative net present value project be worth undertaking because it may open up the way for profitable future investment opportunities. The values of operating and financing flexibilities like the options to expand, defer, or abandon and externally fund a project can be accounted for, an exercise that was not possible under the traditional discounted cash flow methods.

However, many issues remain unresolved as evidenced by recent inability of financial professionals to correlate high tech asset prices with any existing valuation tools, thus raising many questions. In an economy marked by uncertainty, competition and rapid change, how do we value an enterprise in an emerging industry like the Internet or biotechnology? How can we determine the value of a business in a developing or emerging market that is known for its high levels of risk and uncertainty?

This book offers an answer while encouraging further discussions and comments. It puts together many pieces of a puzzle by underscoring key points. First, corporate innovations and technological change are known to be major driving forces of industrial growth. However, it must be understood that growth opportunities are not endowed on companies but are instead acquired through competitive investments. Second, to be able to acquire that opportunity, a firm must win the competitive race, which is riddled with uncertainty. Third, even when the race is won the firm must exercise the option to commercialize the product in order to generate the expected payoff. Financial considerations or changes in the business climate may influence such a decision. Central to all this is the essence of possessing a unique idea to start with, in the first place.

This book should be of interest to both academics and practitioners. For Ph.D. and advanced finance and related courses in capital budgeting, valuation, option theory, cases, and decision analysis the book can serve as a supplementary material. It may be of interest to financial analysts, and executives. Professionals and academics involved in research, investments and financing issues in developing and emerging markets, and the library would also find it a valuable resource.

The contributions of the book are divided into seven chapters. In chapter 1, I present an overview of corporate growth opportunities. I examine valuation issues of intangible growth options while noting that for startup and emerging firms the source of the investment opportunities is primarily internal. I point out the key determinants of the real call option value, including the originality of a unique idea, risk of the venture, financial constraints, competition, speed of innovation, and the magnitude of the potential benefits. Relative weaknesses of the existing valuation models are discussed, highlighting the relevance and advantages of applying real options techniques in pricing growth opportunities.

I then develop the valuation model in chapter 2. I present the model in a competitive game-theoretic setting and allow it to capture three different sources of uncertainty simultaneously. Growth opportunity is modeled as a real call option and R&D is considered the premium paid to hold that option. The capital investment which represents the exercise price of that option; the time when the capital investment is incurred which represents the expiration date; and the potential value of the investment project once it is completed, are all assumed to be uncertain. I incorporate advertising expenditure as the cost of a real exchange option, which enhances the value of the growth opportunities.

Comparative static analysis is conducted in chapter 3. This is mainly qualitative in nature in the sense that I investigate only the direction of change (the sign) in a variable relative to the endogenous variable after disturbing an assumed initial equilibrium. Based on the valuation model the impact on growth opportunities of competition, finance, risk, innovation rents, and the expected time of discovery is examined.

In chapter 4, I carry out a scenario analysis in a case study format of a hypothetical Biotechnology company. A similar analysis could be made for an Internet company. I determine the optimal R&D, the conditional expected time of innovation, and the impact of competition as well as interest rates on R&D. I then compute the value of growth opportunities of the hypothetical company. Advertising expenditure is introduced, and the real exchange option-enhanced value of growth opportunities is derived. I quantify the market value that would have been ignored if traditional discounted cash flow methods were used, given the risk, uncertainty and competition.

In typical emerging market conditions, I discuss the financing of a "stand-alone" growth project in chapter 5. The Binomial Options Pricing Model, a discrete-time analog of the Black-Scholes Options Pricing Theory, is applied. The flexibilities of using debt or equity, altering capital structure, changing debt maturity, defaulting on the project, delaying the project, and expanding the project are evaluated. I also explore the impact of changes in the level of the exercise price on the option value as well as the choice of financing that exercise price.

The empirical analysis follows in chapter 6. I subject the theoretical valuation model to the tests and judge how well it helps us understand and explain reality. I analyze a sample of U.S. publicly traded companies and split them into two groups, the emerging firms and the well-established firms. Cross-sectional regressions are conducted to examine the significance of the relevant variables that spawn the real option. Because of the qualitative differences between assets-in-place and growth opportunities, I investigate if emerging and mature firms behave differently with respect to the predictions of the model.

I summarize the study in chapter 7. I also discuss problems related with data, sample selection and design in the work of this kind. As expected, many questions will linger around the problems associated with determining parameter values if the model is to be used in practice. I briefly explore this area, but shy away from making "specific" claims. Possible avenues for future research are cited.

Throughout the text, although the first person singular is not used, my personal motivation, conviction and views are implied.

Acknowledgements

Many people have helped me in a myriad of ways that made it possible for this book to see the light of day. I owe a special debt to John C. Whitehead for generously supporting my education and for continuing to be a mentor to me. For her enduring guidance, encouragement, love and support, I would especially like to thank Brooke W. Mahoney.

I also benefited enormously from the help and consideration of many friends. Kathleen McCarthy and Susan Berresford provided plugs whenever I was in deficits.

My current and former colleagues deserve special mention for their intellectual guidance. Linda Allen, a superb advisor and chair of my doctoral committee, who was emphatic on the pursuit of excellence and taught me how to pick a tree from the forest. Shulamith Gross, Terry Martell and Kishore Tandon provided their usual warmth and grace.

I would also like to thank participants at the 1997 FMA Conference in Zurich, Switzerland, the 1997 FMA Doctoral Seminar in Honolulu, Hawaii, the 1998 Midwest Finance Association Meetings in Chicago, and workshops at Pace University, University of San Francisco, Hofstra University and Baruch College, for their valuable comments on earlier drafts of the manuscript. A summer research grant from the Lubin School of Business, Pace University, which enabled me complete work on the manuscript is gratefully acknowledged.

Chapter 4 builds on the material also used in Ottoo (1998 (b)). I would like to thank Elsevier Science and the *Quarterly Review of Economics and Finance* for permission to use this material.

I would also like to thank the Assistant Editor, Damon Zucca, and the Production Editor, Nicole Ellis of Garland Publishing Company who worked with me on this book. As expected, my greatest gratitude is to my family. My late parents helped me understand love and perseverance and taught me the value of hard work, discipline, education, and how to give. My brothers and sisters have continued to persevere hardships but understand that there is a time to sow and a time to reap. Most important of all is my daughter Emily Alimo Ottoo, who stands by me enduring late nights and weekends, makes it all worthwhile and ensures that my life is full of love and excitement.

Contents

List of Tables

List of Figures

VALUATION OF CORPORATE GROWTH OPPORTUNITIES

A REAL OPTIONS APPROACH

CHAPTER 1

Growth Opportunities: An Overview

"My great fear is that there are three guys in a garage right now doing the same thing to us that we did to Reuters and Dow Jones."
–Michael R. Bloomberg, Bloomberg Financial Markets, Inc.[1]

1.1 Introduction

Call it "creative destruction." The epitome of the new global economy is the entrepreneurial passion for change. From nations emerging out of centralized planning to the epicenter of global technology - the Silicon Valley, there is an exciting new crop of entrepreneurs who are unleashing a flood of successful new products as well as business models.[2] Companies are being created in record number and at great speed.[3] The old brick-and-mortar corporations are experiencing a shakeout as many are being forced to renew strategies or cannibalize their core business models in order to survive the technological onslaught.

In a recent report, *Fortune* magazine observed that "never before have we seen so many companies explode from birth to market capitalization in the tens of billions of dollars so fast."[4] What is mind-boggling is that these young firms can no longer be judged by the same traditional rules that have been used to evaluate enterprises. The reason is that the basics are lacking. Some of these companies have no factories or profits to report. But they offer one thing nevertheless: growth opportunities.

1

The surge in the number of startup firms coupled with a run up in the prices of their stocks has recently heightened general interest in corporate valuation issues. Most economists in the last five decades upheld the Schumpeterian hypothesis which argues that innovation and technological change are much more likely to come from big business, finding support in the theory of inappropriability and the proven technological breakthroughs by companies like AT&T, Corning and General Electric in transistors, fiber optics and medical imaging. However, there is now a flurry of start-ups and emerging firms that are fueling the emergence of advanced technologies.

In some cases, they have instituted entirely new industries. Twenty years ago, the biotechnology industry hardly existed. Now, it is a multibillion dollar business and firmly established. Then again, witness the emergence of the newest industry, the community of e-corporations, companies built around the Internet which many people now believe is changing the world.

Corporate research and development (R&D) laboratories are now being driven to think more in terms of profit and losses. Companies are gripped by a new wave of dual demand, to introduce quality products and services that consumers can pay for and speed up their delivery to the market. Quality is now defined more by the customer than ever before and is no longer a preserve of an engineer's quality scoreboard. In such an environment, merely possessing economies of scale does not guarantee successful defense of key markets.

Unlike well-established companies, most of the start-up and emerging firms have limited track records, making their valuation very difficult. In finance literature, most businesses are valued as going concerns with the assumption that management is expected to make continued future investments. The level of investment made at each stage of the life of the firm is determined by the net present value that is expected to accrue such that the return on investment exceeds the cost of capital. Investing in positive net present value (NPV) projects thus constitutes a major driving force fueling corporate growth.

However, in a competitive market marked by rapid change and uncertainty, very little is known about valuing corporate growth opportunities. Consider an investment opportunity set available to a firm. If management's decision to invest is discretionary and not automatic then the investment opportunities can only be valuable under certain contingencies and not guaranteed by any asset-in-place. The firm has an option of whether to invest or not. Thus, part of the market value of the firm is accounted for by the present value of future growth opportunities, real options, which can only be acquired if management exercises the option to invest.

Inventions and technological change are the major driving forces of economic and industrial growth. At the individual firm level, this takes the form of investing in positive NPV projects. If firms are viewed as portfolios of real investment opportunities, then the most successful are those with access to the most lucrative projects. As already mentioned, growth opportunities are real growth options whose values are affected by management's strategic investment decisions. Real growth options are not endowed on companies. They are instead acquired through competitive investments. Rather than assuming an exogenously specified distribution of positive NPV projects across firms, this study examines the process of allocation of investment opportunities across firms by valuing basic R&D investment.

The real options literature explores this issue and highlights the under-valuation problem inherent in traditional discounted cash flow (DCF) methods.[5] For any firm, current investments may influence future opportunities either by creating growth opportunities or maximizing the value of an existing opportunity set.

Recent developments in real options pricing have reaffirmed that conventional DCF valuation models tend to ignore the qualitative difference between real growth options and the assets-in-place. The resulting problem is that contractual growth relating to existing assets are erroneously lumped together with strategic growth opportunities arising from financing, investing and operating flexibilities. In a seminal paper, Myers (1977) values growth opportunities as a real call option, while considering the existence of growth opportunities as given. A call option gives its owner the right, but not the obligation, to buy an underlying asset at a specified price on or before a specified date.

We present estimates of the values of intangible assets, or growth opportunities, for selected companies in Table 1.1 below. There is strong evidence that growth opportunities constitute a sizable proportion of the market values of many firms. In financial practice and theory various measures of growth opportunities

Table 1.1. Estimated Values of Growth Opportunities of Selected Companies as at End of December 1998

Industry/Firm	Year Formed	Net Income	Market Value of Equity	Value of Debt	Book Value of Assets	Book Value of Equity	EVF	EVE
Internet:								
Amazon.com	1994	$-124.6	$17,054.8	$ 348.8	$ 648.5	$138.8	96.3%	99.2%
America Online	1985	92.0	68,144.1	372.0	2,214.0	598.0	96.8	99.1
eBay	1995	2.4	9,711.1	0.0	92.5	84.5	99.1	99.1
Biotechnology:								
Genentech	1976	181.9	10,129.5	150.0	2,855.4	2,343.9	72.2	76.9
Amgen	1980	863.2	26,622.0	328.7	3,672.2	2,562.2	86.4	90.4
Biogen	1978	138.7	6,106.2	61.9	924.7	718.6	85.0	88.2
Computer:								
IBM	1914	6,328.0	169,118.3	29,413.0	86,105.0	19,433.0	56.6	88.5
Microsoft	1975	4,490.0	343,534.4	0.0	22,357.0	16,627.0	93.5	95.2
Sun Microsystems	1982	762.9	32,221.4	47.2	5,711.1	3,513.6	82.3	89.1
Pharmaceutical:								
Johnson&Johnson	1886	3,059.0	112,732.3	4,016.0	13,590.0	90,537.3	77.6	87.9
Merck	1908	5,248.2	174,083.3	3,845.0	12,801.8	146,074.9	82.1	92.7
Pfizer	1849	3,351.0	161,751.3	3,256.0	8,810.0	146,705.3	88.9	94.6

Table 1.1. (Continued)

Automotive:								
Ford	1916	22,071.0	71,716.7	132,835.0	237,545.0	23,409.0	−16.1	67.4
General Motors	1908	2,956.0	46,875.3	114,372.0	257,389.0	14,984.0	−59.6	68.0
Navistar Int'l	1902	299.0	1,890.7	2,122.0	6,178.0	769.0	−54.0	59.3
Rubber and Tire:								
Bandag Inc.	1957	59.3	876.9	102.1	755.7	467.3	22.8	46.7
Cooper T&R	1938	127.0	1,549.0	213.7	1,541.3	867.9	12.6	76.6
Goodyear T&R	1898	682.3	7,865.5	1,975.8	10,589.3	3,745.8	−7.6	52.4

Note: All dollar values are in millions. Market value of equity equals market value of common shares plus value of preferred stock. Market value of common is computed as closing stock price times number of outstanding shares. Book value of debt is assumed to be equal to the market value of debt. Debt is long-term debt plus debt in current liabilities. Market value of the firm (assets) equals market value of equity plus value of debt. Excess market value of the firm (EVF) is market value of the firm less book value of assets all divided by market value of the firm. Excess market value of equity (EVE) is derived as market value of equity less book value of equity all divided by market value of equity. EVF and EVE, expressed in percentages, are both measures of growth opportunities.

Source: Compustat PC Plus, Dun & Bradstreet, and author's analysis.

have been used including price-earnings ratio, market-to-book value of equity, Tobin's Q, market-to-book value of assets and the return-on-investment premium over the cost of capital. For our purpose here, we employ excess market-to-book value of assets and excess market-to-book value of equity to demonstrate the existence of growth opportunities in a firm's asset structure.

For a select group of companies, we compute excess market value of assets as a percentage of firm market value (EVF), and excess market value of equity as a percentage of equity market value (EVE) as shown in the last two columns of Table 1.1. The analysis uses annual data and is conducted for a single period ending December 1998. As can be seen, growth opportunities can account for a large portion of a firm's value. For Internet companies, 96 to 99 percent of their market values are accounted for by intangible growth opportunities. Biotechnology, computer and pharmaceutical firms all have very high proportion of growth options. Automotive and rubber and tire companies have relatively lower levels. However, it is highly likely that the market may have factored the potential of the Internet and biotechnology into the pricing of the computer and pharmaceutical firms, respectively.

Table 1.2 shows the changing levels of growth opportunities of IBM from 1979 to 1998. By 1998, IBM was a growth company again after the 1993 turnaround, when it emerged with a strategy to transform itself from a computer giant to a technology and services company driven largely by the Internet. We compare its performance with that of the Dow Jones Industrial Average and the S&P 500 Index in Figure 1.1.

This book melds the real option literature and relevant concepts of traditional valuation analysis by examining the scope of economic interaction between current options and future growth opportunities in risky and competitive environments. Whereas this problem may seem to have limited implications for mature firms, it is critical for start-up ventures where the bulk of market value is in the intangible investment opportunities. For some young companies or in emerging industries, an entire market value of the firm may be due to growth opportunities (see Table 1.1). The capital markets recently have witnessed many technology firms successfully complete their Initial Public Offerings (IPOs) even without demonstrating a history of revenues and earnings.[6]

Table 1.2. Estimated Values of Growth Opportunities of IBM, 1979–1998

Year	Net Income	Market Value of Equity	Value of Debt	Book Value Of Assets	Book Value of Equity	EVF	EVE
1998	$6,328.0	$169,118.3	$29,413.0	$86,100.0	$19,433.0	56.6%	88.5%
1997	6,093.0	100,493.2	26,926.0	81,499.0	19,816.0	36.0	80.3
1996	5,429.0	77,212.1	22,829.0	81,132.0	21,628.0	18.9	72.0
1995	4,178.0	50,306.4	21,629.0	80,292.0	22,423.0	–11.6	55.4
1994	3,021.0	44,277.7	22,118.0	81,091.0	23,413.0	–22.1	47.1
1993	–8,101.0	33,939.3	27,342.0	81,113.0	19,738.0	–32.4	41.8
1992	–4,965.0	28,786.7	29,320.0	86,705.0	27,624.0	–49.2	4.0
1991	–2,827.0	50,820.6	26,947.0	92,473.0	37,006.0	–18.9	27.2
1990	6,020.0	64,567.2	19,545.0	87,568.0	42,832.0	–4.1	33.7
1989	3,758.0	54,093.1	16,717.0	77,734.0	38,509.0	–9.8	28.8
1988	5,806.0	71,875.3	13,380.0	73,037.0	39,509.0	14.3	45.0
1987	5,258.0	68,959.5	5,487.0	63,688.0	38,263.0	14.5	44.5
1986	4,789.0	72,710.8	5,579.0	57,814.0	34,374.0	26.2	52.7
1985	6,555.0	95,697.5	5,248.0	52,634.0	31,990.0	47.9	66.6
1984	6,582.0	75,436.4	4,103.0	42,808.0	26,489.0	46.2	64.9

Table 1.2. (Continued)

Year	Net Income	Market Value of Equity	Value of Debt	Book Value Of Assets	Book Value of Equity	EVF	EVE
1983	5,485.0	74,508.5	3,206.0	37,243.0	23,219.0	52.1	68.8
1982	4,409.0	57,982.8	3,380.0	32,541.0	19,960.0	47.0	65.6
1981	3,308.0	33,687.3	3,442.0	29,586.0	18,161.0	20.3	46.1
1980	3,562.0	39,626.5	2,690.0	26,703.0	16,453.0	36.9	58.5
1979	3,011.0	37,569.5	2,522.1	24,530.0	14,961.2	38.8	60.2

Note: All dollar values are in millions. Market value of equity equals market value of common shares plus value of preferred stock. Market value of common is computed as closing stock price times number of outstanding shares. Book value of debt is assumed to be equal to the market value of debt. Debt is long-term debt plus debt in current liabilities. Market value of the firm (assets) equals market value of equity plus value of debt. Excess market value of the firm (EVF) is market value of the firm less book value of assets all divided by market value of the firm. Excess market value of equity (EVE) is derived as market value of equity less book value of equity all divided by market value of equity. EVF and EVE, expressed in percentages, are both measures of growth opportunities.

Source: Compustat PC Plus and author's analysis.

Figure 1.1 Performance Comparison of IBM Stock Price, IBM Growth Options, Dow Jones Industrial Average and the S&P 500 Index, 1979–1998.

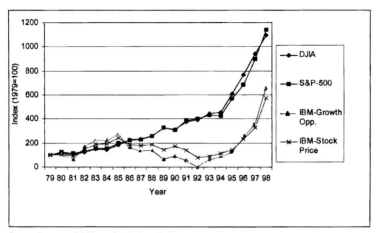

Source: Compustat PC Plus and author's analysis.

Yet they have continued to delight (and baffle) investors with promises of rapid growth, reflected by the run-up in their stock prices.

Which raises a major question: how can we fairly price these young technology companies when traditional and conventional valuation techniques are not applicable?[7] The purpose of this book is to address this problem by focusing on valuation of the growth option component of a firm. Many securities analysts, for instance, have failed to indicate there is any logical connection between the way Internet stocks are priced and conventional techniques of security analysis. In emerging economies where securities markets are underdeveloped or non-existent, such a valuation problem is not new. Because of persistently high levels of uncertainty, generating confidence in applying existing asset-pricing models in these markets is still a far cry.

The sheer lack of a good model for valuing technology stocks should not, however, imply valuation is meaningless. Five years ago Internet stocks were considered "soon-to-burst-bubbles" and "unsafe." Now, foundations, banks, pension funds and a host of other mutual funds hold them in their portfolios. Certainly, the task is daunting, but the need for a good valuation model is compelling.

1.2 Growth Opportunities

1.2.1 Innovation Process

Throughout this book we focus on evaluating the growth option component of an enterprise. We assume that the business entities under consideration have no assets-in-place and no cash flows. All they have is an option to have access to growth opportunities. The model rests on the premise that a firm's objective is to maximize value, which can only be generated by offering quality products or services to the market. However, that process begins with a unique *idea* and concept which must be nurtured or *financed*, all within a very *competitive* and *risky* environment. The introduction of the resulting new product to the market requires *speed*, that is, winning the "competitive race" to innovate.

Thus, the distinction of our model is that it captures the interaction of six key determinants of the value of growth opportunities as illustrated in Figure 1.2: (1) originality of a unique idea (2) risk of the venture (3) competition (4) finances (5) speed of innovation

Figure 1.2 Determinants of Innovation

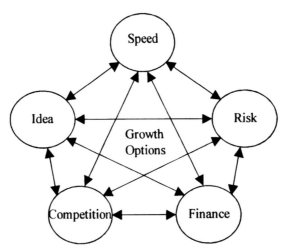

and (6) innovation rents.[8] We believe that these factors characterize the determinants of growth value of firms in emerging industries and markets.

At this juncture, we feel that a brief general description of the model is in order to highlight our motivation. The innovation process proceeds as follows. A firm with an original idea undertakes to make a breakthrough innovation in order to introduce a new product or business model into the market. That idea must be financed, through R&D investments,[9] and the discovery made before a successful rival innovator overtakes the firm and wins. A participating firm is uncertain about both the date of discovery and the identity of the "discoverer." In the model the "discoverer" gains access to productive technology by successfully completing basic R&D projects before its competitors. Thus, its success depends upon winning a competitive race to secure access to these innovation rents. The role of R&D financing is to impact the speed of innovation. Each firm's basic R&D will be affected by the actions of competitive firms. We make an assumption that a firm that loses the competitive race to innovate gets zero value of growth opportunities.

Once a discovery is made the successful firm must decide whether to fund additional investments in order to manufacture the product. Thus, the discovery takes the form of a real option whose value is equal to the expected profits generated by the new product. In order to exercise this real investment option, the firm incurs manufacturing costs, which are unknown a priori and are modeled as the strike price of the option. The magnitude of the strike price is critical in determining the exercise decision of the firm.

There are two implications of capital expenditure. On one hand, it must be paid otherwise all the expected benefits are lost. On the other hand, too high a level may substantially diminish the value of the real growth option. Thus, at time $\tau = 0$, the option premium, the basic R&D expenditure is paid. At an uncertain date $\tau = t>0$, the strike price, the cost of the manufacturing investment is paid. Consequently, innovation (monopoly) rents, which are a function of the size of the premium and patent awarded, are earned. The rents, which are positive if the firm wins but zero if it loses, are valued as an American call option. A one-period investment and production decision strategy is illustrated in Figure 1.3.

Sometimes superior technical innovation and subsequent mass production of the breakthrough product may not be suffi-

Figure 1.3 Investment and Production Decision Tree

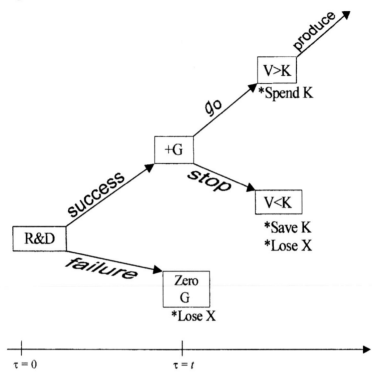

cient. Lack of reliable distribution system and availability of the product in only a few outlets may make its appeal limited. Additional investments in advertising and marketing may be required to open up the market for the new product. In some industries where rapid technological change is common a successful innovator may experience a short head start before the competitors catch up.[10] Thus, investments in marketing and promotional campaign become critical in defending the market. The firm can only choose to incur advertising costs if the enhanced value it expects to generate is greater than the value it would have earned without making this additional expenditure.[11] We therefore model advertising investment as a real exchange option where the original project value is the delivery asset and the enhanced value received is the option asset.[12]

Figure 1.4 Innovation Flow Chart: The Flashlight Model

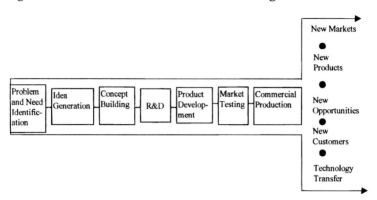

Thus, R&D is essentially a real call option: the underlying asset is the expected value of a completed investment project. Maturity date is the (unknown) date of discovery at which time, the firm simultaneously decides whether to produce. The exercise price is the manufacturing expenditure, which is considered uncertain and may become known as the R&D investments proceed. Volatility of the underlying asset comes from the risk of the expected cash flows from a completed project as well as the uncertainty surrounding the capital investment. In sum, the value of internally generated growth opportunities is modeled as a combination of a real American call option and an exchange option.

1.2.2 Sources of Growth Opportunities

In practice, a firm may tap internal and external sources of growth for purposes of enhancing its market value or achieving diversification. Internally, various options available include R&D investments to roll out new breakthrough products; expansion of distribution and manufacturing capacity to boost sales volume and market share; product pricing to undercut competitors and lift sales; human resource development to position personnel ready for possible new markets, products or techniques; re-invention and brand extension of core products; and restructuring including asset sale, downsizing, and spinoffs to free the company of excess capacity and labor and focus on core operations.

Table 1.3 Examples of Sources of Corporate Growth Opportunities

Investment	Description	Internal or External?	Shared or Proprietary?
Research and Development	R&D Investment is made with the aim of developing new products that may fall into the following categories: a breakthrough new product that will create an entirely new market; radically improved product offering greater perceived value and hence revenues; modified product that provides similar performance or benefit at lower cost; and new brand that will supplement the company's established product lines.[13]	Internal	Proprietary
Mineral Deposits Exploration	A company is granted a lease by a government to explore for a specified type of mineral deposits within a specified time. If a discovery is made, the firm can exercise the option to mine the deposit if the quantity and market price make it viable.	Internal	Proprietary and Shared
Plant Capacity Expansion	Installing a larger plant capacity relative to the size of the existing market in anticipation of a larger market, or a regional economic integration scheme, or an export opportunity arising from dismantling of trade barriers abroad as well as shifts in foreign tastes and demand. A semiconductor firm may boost its production capacity to coincide with potential heavy global demand for memory chips (DRAMS), driven by strong personal computer sales and the trend toward multimedia computing and other functions that require more memory.	External	Shared

Table 1.3 (Continued)

Investment	Description	Internal or External?	Shared or Proprietary?
Acquisitions	A pharmaceutical company acquires a smaller biotech start-up firm with unique gene-splicing techniques rather than developing in-house technology from the ground up, in order to ultimately produce gene-based drugs. Also a multinational airline purchases a local airline in an emerging market to break into a foreign market to increase traffic on potential future routes. The strategic synergies from these two acquisitions, for instance, are expected to be realized from the growth opportunities of the combined firms—through increased upside potential, limited downside risk, lower exercise price, and improved timing of exercise.	External	Shared
New Geographic Market	A multinational company sets up a plant to manufacture a product in a key developing country to capture growth opportunities arising from increased future demand, volatility of exchange rates, and entrenched position against competitors.	External	Shared
Production	A foreign firm newly entering a developing country may sub-contract manufacturing its product to a local producer in the region. The purpose is to delay setting up its own production facilities while studying the market, assembling quality suppliers, and waiting for the economic and political conditions to stabilize.	External	Shared

Table 1.3 (Continued)

Investment	Description	Internal or External?	Shared or Proprietary?
Human Resource Development	Training and motivating personnel on specific technology applications; or making personnel specialize in more than one area of operation in anticipation of an emerging potential product or market. Such investments are valuable since they increase contingency opportunities.	Internal	Proprietary or Shared
Advertising	A firm can be superior in technical innovation, but may be inefficient at marketing the product. It does not follow that a new product can be sold effectively by the current sales force. Investments in advertising is meant to expand distribution of the product, increase its appeal, boost market share, and lift sales.	Internal	Shared or Proprietary
Finance *-Equity Curve-Out*	A parent company offers for sale the equity of a wholly owned subsidiary or division directly to the public. The subsidiary and its core business get external funding plus more exposure to and understanding by the capital markets. While the parent retains majority control, it captures a valuable call option should the new entity appreciate in value in the future.	Internal	Proprietary and Shared

Table 1.3 (Continued)

Investment	Description	Internal or External?	Shared or Proprietary?
-Spin-off	A subsidiary or division of a parent firm is divested and becomes an independent company. The parent firm relinquishes control over the subsidiary. Over time, the new entity develops new investment policies and business strategies different from the original parent, and unlocks value in the stock. Since shares of the new company are distributed on a pro rata basis to existing shareholders of the parent firm, shareholders acquire these growth opportunities.	Internal	Proprietary and Shared
Lobbying	A company successfully lobbies a government that enacts an infant industry protection legislation in its favor. The company buys time; entrenches itself in the market; improves upon its technology and business processes; "evangelizes" its culture; etc., before the legislation expires and competitors swoop in.	Internal	Proprietary and Shared

Externally, a firm may opt for geographical or global expansion; strategic acquisitions and synergistic mergers. Table 1.3 gives brief descriptions of some sources of corporate growth opportunities. An investment that generates proprietary gain or experience places the firm at a competitive advantage against its peers. On the other hand, any technological advance that spills over ends up being "shared" by other firms in the industry. For companies that are growth driven, they might nevertheless proceed with such investments even if it is known apriori that the benefits could be shared by existing and potential competitors.

Whether the source is internal or external, a firm experiences essentially two types of growth in its operating life. The first termed "contractual" or "self-sustaining" refers to opportunities arising from ironclad obligations the firm is required to make in order to earn rates of return above their cost of capital. In essence, contractual growth relates to contributions from existing assets. Prominent adjusted discounted cash flow models[14] that incorporate the component of self-sustaining growth in valuation suggest that if a firm has an opportunity to invest in a project with above normal returns, such investments increase value. Although still generally acceptable, the models fail to recognize that some of these investments are discretionary and so the value of real growth options embedded in real assets of the firm are ignored.

The second type is "strategic growth" generated from real options acquired by making investments that offer potential for future value. Examples of such investment opportunities are listed and described in Table 1.3 above. Strategic growth offers a firm the ability to truncate downside risk while preserving and enhancing upside potential. However, the value of a real growth option can only be captured if the option is exercised.

1.3 Financing Constraints

For start-up and emerging firms, internal sources of growth seem to be the only feasible option. Because of age, financial constraint and limited size of operating capacity an emerging firm may not have the capability to purchase and integrate outside technology or business, or engage in extensive expansion geographically as a viable means of achieving growth. Internet stocks whose hyper-valuations have given them the currency to make rapid acquisitions to build market share while running deeper deficits have been the exception. For simplicity, we ignore these sequential possibilities for a while, and assume that none of the external options are readily available to the firm, except internally engaging in basic R&D investments in order to introduce a new product or process to the market. We thus posit that internal capital is the optimal mode of financing that option.

If stock market investors are not myopic and focus on long-term performance then it would seem that the intangible assets are valued by the market and are reflected in the measured capital of the firm. Basic R&D projects are by definition uncertain. A firm is simultaneously uncertain whether it or its competitors will succeed in making the innovation. By sustaining R&D investments, competing firms hope to acquire better estimates of future states of nature that would determine their resulting payoffs. However, at each stage, managers of a firm may have more information than competitors and capital markets, and different firms may have different information about which states will occur. Thus, information asymmetry may impact the source and cost of financing.

It is highly likely that the extent to which real growth options constitute the market value of the firm may influence its mode of financing. However, puzzling as capital structure issues still are, it is unclear if there is an optimal financing policy for growth options. It may be implied from Diamond (1989) that start-ups and emerging firms with little reputation have less access to external debt than are well established firms. This conforms to Jensen and Meckling (1976), Myers (1977), and Stulz (1990) who show that leverage is expected to be negatively associated with the extent of growth opportunities. The view of Stulz (1990) is that volatility of cash flows has a strong effect on financing policy of a firm since it increases the agency costs of managerial discretion. Managerial discretion induces two cost components. One is an over-investment cost caused by management investing too much in some circumstances, and the other is the under-investment cost that arises because of management's lack of credibility when it claims available internal funds are not sufficient to exhaust all positive NPV projects.

Stulz argues that a solution to the agency problem of managerial discretion is to make it less likely that resources available to management will differ significantly from the resources stockholders expect management to have. The desire to achieve a decrease in the dispersion of cash flow and to re-align the expectation of investors with the investment and financing strategies of management may explain why some firms, especially young ones, defer making dividend payments.

Also, because of informational heterogeneity across investor groups, the capital markets will fail to instantaneously aggregate information about a firm. Thus, investors cannot properly identify the relative performance of firms engaged in a competitive race to innovate merely by observing their market prices. Because information acquisition is a costly activity, investors will consequently price their own capital very highly for any needy firm that approaches the market. This may lead some good firms to pass up positive NPV projects.

Management of an established company realizes this and most likely would desire to separate itself from the rest. It would choose to use an unambiguous signal to convey to the market that it has a stable expected set of cash flows sufficient to meet debt obligations as well as dividend payments without triggering undue stress on the financial condition of the firm. One such unique signaling device is dividend payment. Start-up firms cannot mimic this signal because they lack the stability and necessary level of cash flows to back it up. In addition, mimicking a mature firm would be expensive since higher costs of issuing equity or debt to pay cash dividends must be incurred.[15] Also, seeking external capital brings with it the amount and intensity of capital markets scrutiny, which a start-up firm may not desire.

It turns out that a firm will know more about the prospect of its R&D investment than the investors will. Due to the resulting information asymmetry, credit rationing[16] may ensue and the market may fail to finance basic R&D of emerging firms to the levels needed to compete for the monopoly rents. Access to internal sources of financing, as in Myers' "Pecking-Order" theory (1984) and Myers and Majluf's benefit of financial slack (1984), become a binding constraint for these companies, even though internal cash flows might generate Jensen's (1986) free cash flow problems. If internal funds are lacking, and there is no access to external capital either, then the firm fails to enter the strategic growth competition. Therefore, we argue that internally generated cash flow is a more important determinant of firm value for emerging than for mature firms.

In the empirical analysis of this study, we recognize dividend payment as a signaling device and utilize it to distinguish an emerging from a mature firm.[17] Thus, an emerging firm is one that is relatively young and has never issued cash dividends over its entire life.

1.4 Basic Approaches to Valuation

Thus far, we have discussed the critical issues of investment decisions under uncertainty while motivating the purpose and direction of this book. As pointed out earlier, one of the major challenges in the business world is the task of measuring the value of a business segment, a particular asset, or the entire enterprise. The problem may stem from the choice of a valuation model, the effectiveness of the model, or the difficulty that changing asset conditions, business scenarios, and economic environments impart on the feasibility of the model. In keeping with this tradition we'll now revisit the topic, as a matter of emphasis, before proceeding to formally develop the valuation model in the next chapter.

There are three basic types of business valuation techniques that are often applied: (i) the discounted cash flow method, (ii) the relative measures, and (iii) the contingent claims models.

1.4.1 The Discounted Cash Flow Method

The DCF method requires forecasting the free cash flows to the enterprise and discounting them to the present at an appropriate risk-adjusted cost of capital. As already discussed, DCF has many limitations when faced with evaluating embedded growth options. First, DCF fails to capture the value of managerial flexibilities and strategic decisions such as the option to expand, delay, abandon, or switch investments. Second, for a firm with a large component of growth opportunities, the potential cash flow (or the value of the underlying asset) is very volatile. The volatility of the cash flows demands a difficult and imprecise task of deriving equilibrium risk premiums, which must be added to the risk-free rate to determine the appropriate discount rate.

Third, because of the characteristics of the growth options, cash flows exhibit non-linear behavior. Thus, the usual exercise in DCF of computing expected cash flows becomes a problem and, at its worst, meaningless. Fourth, DCF is unable to make time-series links across projects and the impact of a project on future investment opportunities is not accounted for. Finally, DCF analysis is linear and static in nature and assumes growth opportunities either are not totally reversible or are a now-or-never opportunities.[18]

1.4.2 Valuation by Multiples

The relative valuation technique on the other hand employs ratio analysis to determine the relative value of a company in question. The multiples widely used include price-earnings (P/E), market-to-book value of assets (M/BV), price-to-sales (P/S), and price-to-EBITDA.[19] For example, an analyst can express the price of a stock of uBid.com the Internet company, as:

Price of uBid = P_{uBid} = $(P/E)_{Comp} \times E_{uBid}$ where $(P/E)_{Comp}$ is the average P/E ratio of comparable firms-companies in the same industry and belonging to the same risk class as uBid.com. As is evident, this model immediately breaks down if there is no "E" (or "S") or if "E" is negative for the company to be valued, a typical scenario for most enterprises at early stages of development. Also, the choice of comparable firms may be fraught with error, and how perfect $(P/E)_{Comp}$ measures $(P/E)_{uBid}$ is questionable. The implicit assumption here is that the growth rate of expected earnings or sales of uBid.com is equivalent to that of the comparable firms, an unlikely possibility. Furthermore, large-scale averaging of variables of the comparable firms may introduce a higher degree of error into the model.

1.4.3 Contingent Claims Models

Contingent claims valuation approach is more in line with the direction of this book. These models have been shown to resolve many of the shortcomings of DCF methods in evaluating growth opportunities. The continuous-time real growth option models,[20] for instance, assume the value of the completed project follows a lognormal distribution, which implies the returns are normally distributed, thereby permitting a non-stochastic discounting framework. The lognormality property captures the notion that growth opportunities exhibit claims that are not symmetric, and whose discount rates vary in a complex manner over time. Also, Cox, Ross and Rubinstein (1979) suggested the binomial tree method, a good discrete-time approximation of the Black-Scholes continuous-time model.

However, existing real options valuation models still suffer from a number of drawbacks, including inappropriate model assumptions, poor estimation procedures, and the difficulty faced in capturing more than one source of uncertainty at a time. These problems have limited their wider applications. Notwithstanding these weaknesses, contingent claims analysis has opened up more avenues than any other technique for modeling valuation of intangible assets as well as evaluating the interaction of strategic investments. In the next chapter, we develop one such model for valuing corporate growth opportunities.

1.5 CONCLUSION

Growth opportunities account for a large portion of assets of many firms, especially start-up and emerging companies. The primary source of these investment opportunities for young firms is internal. The success of this entrepreneurial venture seems to hinge on six key variables: originality of a unique idea; risk of the venture; financing; competition; speed of innovation and potential benefits. Conventional Capital budgeting tools based on discounted cash flows are inherently inadequate in valuing these intangible assets. Real options pricing models, which incorporate sources of uncertainty and assume no symmetry of potential cash flows, provide a better approach. In the next chapter we contribute to the field of corporate valuation by developing a unique real options model, which captures the characteristics of growth opportunities.

NOTES

1. *Business Week,* January 11, 1999.
2. Electronic-commerce is considered a new business model.
3. *Business Week,* August 25, 1997, page 66.
4. See *Fortune,* May 24, 1999, page 110.
5. See Myers (1977); Brennan and Schwartz (1985); Majd and Pindyck (1987); Trigeorgis and Mason (1987); Kester (1993); and Trigeorgis (1993).

6. On November 11, 1998, Earth Web Inc. went public on the Nasdaq Stock Market closing at \$48.6875 from an offering price of \$14, even when the company had not made a single dollar of profit, and despite a clear warning that "the company anticipates that it will continue to incur net loses for the foreseeable future," in its prospectus (*Wall Street Journal,* November 12, 1998).

7. Price-to-sales ratio is the current yardstick of choice in Silicon Valley to gauge the power of a given tech company (See the discussion in Moore (1998)).

8. Economists define "rent" as payment for the use of factors of production that are fixed in supply.

9. Our notion of R&D here includes all operating costs plus the market value of the compensation foregone by an entrepreneur who chooses to work in own garage in hopes of launching a new product.

10. A biotech firm may introduce a pill with a superior claim of none of the side effects of an existing competing drug, thus snatching away some market share of the earlier arrival. Sepracor Inc. was to introduce a purified version of Prozac, Eli Lilly's blockbuster antidepressant drug that generates between \$1.5bn and \$2.3bn in annual sales and is soon coming off-patent. Late 1998, Lilly struck a deal with Sepracor to co-develop the new Prozac that will now enjoy patent protection until the year 2015 (see the *Wall Street Journal,* June 12, 1996 and *Busines Week,* January 11, 1999).

11. A successful smaller biotech firm often lines up a major drug marketing power house like Glaxo, Merck, Bristol-Myers Squibb, Pfizer, Eli Lilly, etc. to co-market its product (see *Business Week,* January 11, 1999). Analysts also credit the near-dominance of Yahoo! and Amazon.com brand names to the boost in their advertising (*Business Week,* September 7, 1998 and December 14, 1998).

12. See Carr (1988).

13. See Kotler, Philip, 1994 "Marketing Management," 8th edition. Prentice Hall, page 316.

14. For instance, Miller and Modigliani (1961) and Gordon (1955, 1967).

15. For an excellent exposition on signaling theory, see Ross (1977), Bhattacharya (1979), Myers and Majluf (1984), Miller and Rock (1985), and John and Williams (1985). Jensen and Meckling (1976) argue that because of the agency cost of equity, firms may shy away from using equity just for the sake of raising funds to pay dividends. Tax-based dividend signaling models postulate that dividends only convey information about a firm's values because of the higher tax they impose on shareholders.

Using data on Germany where dividends are not tax-disadvantaged, Amhiud and Murgia (1997) find that stock price response to dividend news in Germany is similar to that documented in the U.S., suggesting that besides taxes, dividends are informative. It is agreed that where corporate managers have greater discretion in accounting reporting, financial statement variables may even be less informative about current and potential earnings of the firm than signaling devices like dividends. To new suppliers of capital, for instance, audited financial statements may not adequately communicate every relevant information, especially "adverse" news about the firm.

16.   In competitive capital markets, credit rationing takes the form of raising the cost of capital.

17.   [We recognize the controversy that may surround this choice]. Masulis and Trueman (1986) state that firms with many growth opportunities will use all their internally generated funds without paying dividends, but established firms will pay out dividends because not all internal resources will be exhausted by investment opportunities. Pilotte (1992) also employs this criterion in an event-study of stock price reaction to new financing.

18.   See Lander and Pinches (1998).

19.   EBITDA stands for Earnings Before Interests, Taxes, Depreciation and Amortization.

20.   For a good survey of continuous-time and non-continuous-time option pricing models, refer to Lander and Pinches (1998). Also see Trigeorgis (1995).

CHAPTER 2
The Valuation Model

"Speed is the name of the game."
–Fortune Magazine[1]

2.1 Investment Decision

2.1.1 R&D Information Structure

We model an emerging firm as one purchasing a basic R&D option to develop a new technology or product. Basic R&D option is the option that gives the firm the right to make positive NPV investments if and when the R&D project is successfully completed. The intention here is not to draw a formal distinction between "basic" and "applied" R&D[2]. We assume that the innovation the firm would make is not an end-use product but a product or process that will lead to further generic or targeted product or process developments.

Figure 1.4 in Chapter 1 illustrates how a single breakthrough innovation can result in multiple opportunities. In real options theory we refer to such an outcome as a compound option, which is defined as an option that creates other options when it is exercised. Recent developments have shown that rapid advances in business technology give rise to additional benefits to the extent that they spur demand by broadening applications. In our model, the granting of patents[3] that provide monopoly rents to the firm exercising the real option captures the potential value resulting from additional products, markets and opportunities.

27

We suppose that there are two startup firms in the same industry that engage in R&D investments to develop a unique product in order to fulfill an identified need in the market. The R&D project is assumed to have a finite life since such opportunities can be captured by a competitor or diminished by introduction of a substitute. We present a two-firm model to simplify the analysis without any loss of generalities. A discussion of the general *N*-firm framework, and the variations of the investment strategies under monopoly and cartel forms of market structure, is given in Chapter 3 and the Appendix. We consider a simplified information structure in which the firms are of two types. Firm *H* is assumed to be a high-type company in the sense that it is capable of producing superior R&D performance. Firm *L*, on the other hand, is considered a low-type. It is further assumed that each firm does not know its own relative identity or the identity of the competitor. However, in every period, the level of R&D outlays of any firm is common knowledge.

The objective of R&D project managers is to maximize the net information value of R&D investment period by period, consistent with their budgetary allocation schedules. Net information value, referred to here as information value added (IVA), is the difference between the value generated from the information captured from undertaking the project and the cost incurred in acquiring that information. It is understood that the larger the amount of IVA generated the higher the probability of making a discovery. We don't factor in a parameter for reward or penalty in the model but assume that managers are incented by positive IVA, which they strive to maximize, and are demotivated by an information value gap (negative IVA).

Consider a one-period decision plan. The net information value of R&D investment for any firm *i* is expressed as:

$$V_1 = \int_{s=0}^{\infty} p_1(s)\Big[\tilde{V}_1(s,x)\Big]ds - X_1 \tag{1}$$

where *i* = *H*, *L*. *p*(*s*) represents the information value at state *s* of a unit of payoff resulting from the cost of effort. $\tilde{V}(s,x)$ denotes the total payoff due to the effort committed. And *X* represents the cost of effort, which is the R&D expenditure.

We assume that $p_H > p_L$. Also, $\dfrac{d\tilde{V}}{dX} > 0$, implying that expending that effort is valuable; and $\dfrac{d^2\tilde{V}}{dX^2} < 0$, implying the value of that effort declines. p can be considered the price of private (inside) information. It may also be taken to represent the probability of generating value information from a set of raw information.[4]

Think of researchers in a scientific laboratory. A continuous thought process toward a discovery often governs their actions. Suppose we break down that process into simple discrete units of time. The ultimate goal of every research team is to reach that "eureka" moment of innovation. Every period, the team would assess its effort, measured by how much valuable "confidential" information has been generated. We illustrate this concept by use of Figure 2.1 below to help visualize the dynamic search for value. As an example, suppose there are three possible outcomes of the R&D commitment each period, given a state of nature. Outcome 1 implies that firm i has captured new and valuable information. Outcome 2 implies new information has been generated but none of it is of any value to the project. The third outcome signifies no new information is gathered, despite the effort put in.

Note that $\tilde{a}_1$, $\tilde{a}_2$ and $\tilde{a}_3$ are the probability weights of the outcomes whose integral over all possible states of nature would give rise to the instantaneous probability of success p_i. In other words, p_i is a function of $\tilde{a}_1$, $\tilde{a}_2$ and $\tilde{a}_3$. The best scenario for firm i is to have $\tilde{a}_1$ as large as possible and $\tilde{a}_3 = 0$. Of course, the unfavorable case is if $\tilde{a}_3 > \tilde{a}_2$ and $\tilde{a}_1 = 0$. It turns out that even if two firms spend equal amount of money in R&D in a given period, their levels of p

Figure 2.1 Representation of Probability Weights

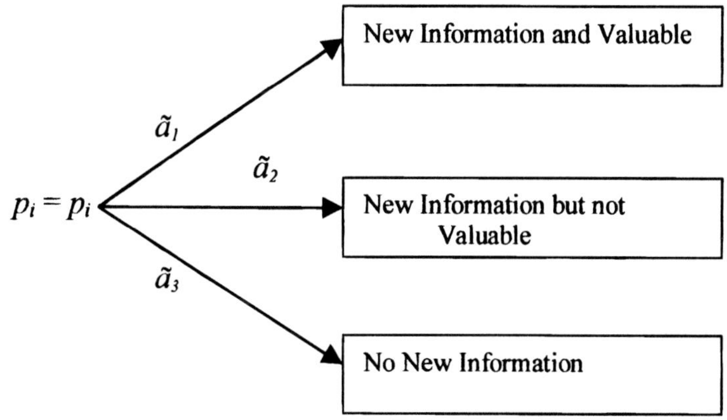

would not necessarily be equal because of the relative differences in $\tilde{a}_1$, $\tilde{a}_2$ and $\tilde{a}_3$.

In the New World of technology driven businesses, there is overwhelming pressure on corporate managers for quality recruiting. The goal is to assemble a pool of talent that can generate and sustain a higher level of p than any competitors. In reality when the challenge looks unbearable for a single firm, it may seek a partner or two to collaborate on a particular venture to battle competitors. Alternatively, a company may make strategic acquisitions to bolster its technological prowess. The aim is to eliminate cost overlaps and avoid duplication of efforts in order to raise the level of research efficiency. For instance, IBM, Motorola and Apple Computer teamed up to develop Power PC chip. In response, Intel and Hewlett-Packard joined to compete with them to develop a chip that would run a wide variety of machines, including PCs, workstations and file servers[5] (see Table 2.1 below for more examples of corporate R&D collaborations). However, not all collaborations do succeed as partners may feud over strategy, financing and technology. Also, a firm might be forced to engage in licensing since a tech product may require several parts and linkages, and turning out these parts in-house could be costly and time-consuming.

As we have already stated, suppose both firms commit the same level of R&D, such that $X_H = X_L$. Then given the same states of nature, $V_H > V_L$. We argue that it is not possible that a low-type firm might mimic a high-type by spending more in R&D in order to signal that it has a higher IVA. The reason is that if R&D market is competitive and $p_H > p_L$, then since firm H has a higher "technical skill" in capturing information and turning it into value, it would be willing to pay more for that information than firm L. In other words, for firm L, more information is being generated but proportionately less in value is captured since $\dfrac{d^2\tilde{V}}{dX^2} < 0$, thereby creating a value-gap, which is a disincentive for the managers.

Thus, for firm L there is no reward for mimicking firm H by spending too much in R&D. In practice, corporate labs understand that without the right idea to begin with, there is really no compelling need to move fast. The objective of management is to maximize V_i with respect to the cost of effort X_i, such that $\dfrac{\partial V_i}{\partial X_i} = V_i' - 1 = 0$, giving $V_i' = 1$ as the first-best solution. In the next

Table 2.1 Examples of Corporate R&D Collaborations

Collaboration	Companies	Project
1.	Warner-Lambert Co. Pfizer, Inc.	Teamed up in 1997 to introduce Liptor, a cholesterol-reducing drug that rivals Zocor, produced by Merck.
2.	Gilead Sciences, Inc. Roche Holdings, Ltd.	Developed GS4104, an experimental drug that can significantly reduce the length and severity of a flu attack, first pill to effectively shorten a flu bout caused by both major strains of the influenza virus.
3.	IBM Sears Roebuck & Co. CBS, Inc.	Formed Prodigy, the Internet-services company, in a $1 billion joint venture in 1984.
4.	Eli Lilly & Co. Sepracor, Inc.	Struck a deal to develop a new version of Prozac, with fewer side and interactions effects, to enjoy patent protection till year 2015, relieving the revenue pressure on Eli whose old Prozac was coming off patent.
5.	Synaptic Pharmaceutical Co. Eli Lilly & Co.	Synaptic signed R&D deal late 1991 to provide its gene-splicing techniques in support of Eli's Central Nervous System research to help deliver drugs precisely to where they are needed in the brain.
6.	IBM Siemens (Germany) Toshiba (Japan)	Teamed up to develop 256-megabit memory chips.

Table 2.1 (Continued)

Collaboration	Companies	Project
7.	General Motors Corp. Ford Chrysler Corp.	Formed 12 consortiums on such topics as: electric-vehicle batteries; parts recycling; better crash dummies; and setting wiring standards throughout the industry to reduce from existing 100 different wiring connectors to fewer than 10.
8.	Canon Hewlett-Packard	Joined to make laser printers. Canon to provide printer heads, and Hewlett-Packard to handle software, micro-controllers, customer research and marketing.
9.	Daimler-Benz (Germany) Ballard Power Systems (Can.)	To co-develop a fuel-cell-powered vehicle.
10.	Lanxide Corp. Alcan Aluminium (Canada)	Joined in ceramics materials research. To make tools and other products that must withstand abrasion.
11.	Sulzer Brothers Ltd. (Switz.) Toyoda Automatic Loom Works (Japan)	Joint venture for the development and production of air-jet weaving machines.

Source: Business Week (October 12, 1998; June 27, 1994; and October 25, 1991); *The Wall Street Journal* (September 25 and 28, 1998).

sub-section we develop a dynamic model of R&D investments and re-affirm that the objective of management is to maximize the net present value of the R&D project, which is analogous to the objective of maximizing the information value added.

2.1.2 R&D Investment Dynamics

Determining R&D choice with rivalry proceeds along a non-cooperative game model[6]. We suppose that a flow of benefits from R&D investments becomes available only to the first firm to succeed in making the innovation. R&D investments are initiated at time $\tau = 0$. The first firm is expected to succeed at some time $\tau = t$ $(0 < t < T)$. We assume that if no discovery is made by time T then all benefits related to the R&D investments will vanish. Each firm, however, is uncertain about the date of innovation $(t < T)$ by itself or by the competitor. R&D investments span over time $\tau = 0, 1, 2, \ldots, t, \ldots,$ T, where t represents the discovery date of the winning firm and T denotes the maximum time to innovation.

Once the R&D is successful at time t and the new product is tested and introduced, the successful firm must decide whether to manufacture the product for commercialization. If the firm decides to, it will incur a manufacturing cost $K(t)$, in order to realize V_1, the present value of the stream of uncertain future cash flows to be generated by this investment. For any firm i, V_1 represents the market value of a contingent claim on the stream of net cash flows that arise from installing the manufacturing plant subsequent to the discovery at time t. It is recognized that if $K(t) > V_1$, the firm will not manufacture the product and the growth value will be lost.

A participating firm can assess $K(\tau)$, the required capital investments, at $\tau = 0$. However, $K(t)$ is uncertain since new information is revealed over the basic R&D investment period between dates $\tau = 0$ and t. We consider the manufacturing investment, the strike price of the option, a stochastic variable[7]. R&D investment is thus a real growth option on the value of a completed manufacturing project as the underlying asset; the capital cost $K(t)$, as exercise price; time of innovation t, as maturity date; and the R&D outlays X, as the cost of or premium on this option. Thus, at time t, the firm's investments payoff is $max[V_1 - K(t), 0]$.

Assume a market in which the two firms[8] compete for an amount of benefit $V(t)$, that can only be available to the firm that first introduces a product at some date t. The winner would immediately receive a patent protection to guarantee to it the flows of benefits indefinitely. Spillover effects are ruled out and a belated rival innovator would get zero benefit. In order to reap the expected benefits, firm H must commit to an R&D level X_H. Similarly, X_L represents R&D outlays for firm L. The investments in information acquisition will continue until any one of the two firms succeeds.

At anytime $\tau \leq t$, firm H, just like firm L, is faced with two kinds of uncertainty. First, it has no knowledge of the exact date it will succeed in making a discovery[9]. Essentially, for both firms H and L, the R&D is paying for a random variable $\tau_H(X_H)$ and $\tau_L(X_L)$, respectively, representing an uncertain date at which the R&D project would be successful. So, maximizing the value of R&D project is tantamount to reducing the variance of the distributions of τ_H and τ_L.

The second type of uncertainty is exogenous in nature. Each firm is unaware of the introduction date of its rival. We denote this uncertainty, from firm H's perspective, by a random variable $\tau_H(X_L)$ representing the uncertainty firm L also faces about when it will successfully make the innovation[10].

Under the assumption of rational expectations,

$$\tau_H(X_L) = \tau_L(X_L) \tag{2}$$

That is, the uncertainty firm H faces about when firm L might innovate is equivalent to the uncertainty firm L has about its own date of discovery.

Thus, the condition that $\tau_H(X_H) < \min[\tau_L(X_L), T]$ must be satisfied for firm H to succeed before firm L. Throughout the analysis, we examine the competitive race from firm H's perspective for tractability. Under the assumption that each firm's discovery time t follows an exponential distribution we have, for firm H,

$$Prob\big(\tau_H(X_H) \leq t\big) = 1 - e^{-f(X_H)t} \tag{3}$$

Suppose for a moment that firm H has no competition in the market. We derive the expectation of this random variable by applying the procedure of integration by parts (see Appendix I) to give:

$$E[\tau_H(X_H)] = \frac{1}{f(X_H)} \qquad (4)$$

representing the expected time of innovation for firm H as a monopoly company in the industry. $f(X_H)$ is the constant hazard rate of success for firm H and is considered only a function of X. It is the conditional probability that firm H will introduce a new product to the market at any subsequent date. We make the usual assumptions often made in optimal time models, that the function $f(X)$ is twice continuously differentiable and that it satisfies the following boundary conditions: $f(0) = 0$; $f'(X) = 0$ as $X \to \infty$; and $f''(X) < 0$, so as to allow for initially increasing returns to X, with possibly diminishing returns eventually.

Now, introduce firm L into play. From Equations 2 and 3 it follows that

$$Prob[\tau_H(X_t) \le t] = 1 - Prob[\tau_t(X_t) > t] = 1 - e^{-f(X_L)^t} \qquad (5)$$

Therefore, the probability that firm H introduces the product by time t before firm L has done so, is computed (see Appendix II) as:

$$\left(\frac{f(X_H)}{f(X_L) + f(X_H)} \right) \left(1 - e^{-t[f(X_L) + f(X_H)]} \right) \qquad (6)$$

Thus, from (6), the present value of the benefits $V(t)$ that firm H will receive on successfully completing the R&D project before firm L, is given as:

$$E\left[V(t) \,|\, \{\tau_H(X_H) \le (\tau_L(X_L), t)\} \right]$$

$$= \int_0^\infty V(t) dP[X_H \le X_L \wedge t] e^{-rt} \, dt$$

$$= \int_0^\infty V(t) \left[f\left(X_H e^{-l[f(X_H)+f(X_H)]} \right) e^{-rt} \right]$$

$$= \frac{V(t) f(X_H)}{f(X_L) + f(X_H) + r} \qquad (7)$$

where r is the discount rate and t is the conditional expectation of $\tau_H(X_H)$. The expected value of t, the expectation of $\tau_H(X_H)$, is therefore determined as (see Appendix III):

$$E(\tau) = \frac{f(X_H)}{\left[f(X_L) + f(X_H)\right]^2} \tag{8}$$

Equation (8) states that the expected time of discovery for firm H is a product of its own hazard rate and the inverse of a squared sum of the hazard rates of both firms H and L, which are in turn a function of the R&D of the two firms under competition[11]. Note that t is the observed value of τ.

The application of the exponential distribution to determine the minimum time to innovate permits a major advantage of the distribution by its memory-less property. It implies that the probability of arrival of new valuable (and strategic) information does not depend on the arrival of past valuable information. For instance, if a firm has not yet made a discovery by time t, the probability that it would succeed any time between t and the maximum date T, is the same as its initial probability of success before t. In other words, the distribution of R&D investments after time t is the same as the original distribution if no innovation is observed by that date.

R&D project has been assumed to have a finite life. This assumption may be relaxed while determining the conditional expected time of innovation, without loss of results. Rational expectations hypothesis is also assumed to hold such that each firm's expectations about the action of the competitor is correct.

2.2 Production Decision

2.2.1 Exercising the Real Call Option

In the previous section, we argued that on the date of discovery t, management of the successful firm would have an option to mass-produce the technological product. It should be emphasized that even if a firm wins the competitive race to innovate and is granted a patent on this date, the acquisition of growth opportunities is not guaranteed. We rule out licensing options. Any innovating firm needs to be warned that basking in the glory of a breakthrough discovery by itself is not sufficient. The firm must always execute. In emerging industries that are driven heavily by technological advances, it is speed, innovation and successful execution of the production process that count.

If firm H wins, the R&D level X_H would be the optimal level required being successful. In order to capture the value of growth opportunities it must then go ahead and make the required capital investments to manufacture the new product thereby exercising a real call option on the value of the investment V_1^{12}, with capital expenditure $K(t)$ as strike price. The real call option has the following payoff:

$$max[V_1(t) - K(t), O] \qquad (9)$$

We assume that the expected value of the project cash flows V_1 follows a diffusion process[13]:

$$dV_1 = \alpha_v V_1 dt + \sigma_v V_1 dz_v \qquad (10)$$

where: α_v is the instantaneous expected return on the project,
σ_v^2 is the instantaneous variance of the return, and
dz_v is the Gauss-Wiener process, defining the uncertainty underlying the process (10).

As discussed earlier, when a firm initiates R&D investment at $\tau = 0$, it estimates $K(0)$ which is known but is understood to vary subsequent to $\tau = 0$. However, the relevant manufacturing costs paid to exercise the option at date t is $K(t)$, which is uncertain any time before t occurs. If the level of $K(t)$ is prohibitively high, a successful firm may be forced to let the option expire unexercised. A company may remain unfazed by the innovation success of its competitor and would still desire or facilitate a capital constraint on the potential manufacturer to thwart its move. On the other hand, *ceteris paribus,* a low level of required capital is a boon to the winner's value of the growth option[14].

Overall, it turns out that the payoff from undertaking this production depends on the changes in value of the manufacturing project as well as on the variation in the uncertain strike price, itself correlated with the process of V_1. Thus, we assume the exercise price has the following dynamics:[15]

$$dK = \alpha_k K dt + \sigma_k K dz_k \qquad (11)$$

where: α_k is the instantaneous expected rate of increase of the exercise price;

σ_k^2 is the instantaneous variance of the exercise price; and

dz_k is the standard Wiener process.

We suppose that the Wiener processes, dz_v and dz_k, have an instantaneous correlation coefficient σ_{vk}, where $dz_v dz_k = \sigma_{vk} dt$. The resulting real option is a call option on an asset with a stochastic strike price. Fischer (1978) shows that the value of such an option could be derived by purchasing a hedge security to hedge against changes in the exercise price to provide insurance against unanticipated changes in $K(t)$. Fischer demonstrates that for this to be appropriate the stochastic percentage changes in the value of the hedge security be perfectly correlated with the stochastic component of the percentage changes in the strike price. Thus, the expected rate of return α_h, on the hedge security is equivalent to the risk-free rate of interest plus the risk premium on the hedge security. Under perfect capital market assumptions, the expected rate of return on this hedge security equals the cost of hedging. The present value of the benefits from innovation and successful execution of the production process that firm H would receive at time t is therefore:

$$V(t) = V_1 N(d_1) - K(0) N(d_2) e^{-t(\alpha_h - \alpha_k)} \qquad (12)$$

where: $d_1 = \dfrac{\ln \dfrac{V_1}{K(0)} + (\alpha_h - \alpha_k + \dfrac{\sigma^2}{2})t}{\sigma \sqrt{t}}$

$d_2 = d_1 - \sigma \sqrt{t}$

$\sigma^2 = \text{Variance} \left(\dfrac{d[(\dfrac{V_1}{K(\tau)})] / (\dfrac{V_1}{K(\tau)})}{dt} \right) = \sigma_v^2 + \sigma_k^2 - 2\sigma_{vk}\sigma_v\sigma_k$

and N(.) is the cumulative standard normal density function.

R&D costs X_H and X_L will be incurred so long as no firm has made a breakthrough discovery or until any of the firms has succeeded. For firm H this flow of expenditure will occur with probability density $[f(X_H) + f(X_L)] (e^{-t[f(X_L) + f(X_H)]})$. Hence, the expected value of R&D outlays is given as:

$$\int_0^\infty \left[[f(X_H) + f(X_L)]e^{-t(f(X_H)+f(X_L))}(\int_0^t X_H e^{-r\tau}d\tau) \right] dt$$

(13)

$$= \frac{X_H}{[f(X_H) + f(X_L) + r]}$$

That is, the present value of R&D spending is computed as the R&D outlays discounted by the sum of the relative probabilities of innovation and the risk-free rate of interest. The problem of firm H is to choose the level of R&D that maximizes the NPV of the expected benefits from the new product. Thus, its objective function is to:

$$maximize\left[PV(R \& D \text{ project}) - PV(R \& D \text{ cost})\right]$$

$$= maximize \frac{V(t)f(X_H) - X_H}{[f(X_H) + f(X_L) + r]}$$

(14)

Suppose $X_H = X_H^*$ is the solution for Equation 14 guaranteeing the optimal net benefits, and G_X is the value of the real growth option given by Equation 7. Substituting for $V(t)$ in Equation 12 and using the expected value of t defined by Equation 8, gives:

$$G_X = \frac{f(X_H)}{f(X_L) + f(X_H) + r} \left\{ V_1 N(d_1) - K(0)N(d_2)e^{-t(\alpha_h - \alpha_k)} \right\}$$

(15)

Equation 15 is the valuation model of corporate innovation, a measure of the market value of a firm without consideration of existing assets or market making.

2.3 Marketing Decision

To capture a wider consumer market and subsequently generate larger revenues from this new product, we assume that the firm must commit to additional expenditures on advertising and developing the distribution network. The reason is that even if a product has already been developed, its market has not. Prices and other conditions in the factor and product markets may change as news of the new product is analyzed. As a result, the firm may have to commit some funds for advertising and marketing in order to make and facilitate the market. The firm can only choose to incur marketing costs if the benefit it generates consequently is higher than the benefit it would have earned without this additional expenditure[16].

We suppose that the firm would spend M in expectation of receiving a higher present value of cash flows of V_2 (net of M), where $V_2 > V_1$. V_2 is defined similar to V_1. Certainly, V_2 depends on V_1 and hence, on the success of the R&D investment. V_2 also follows a stochastic process with return α_2, volatility σ_2, and dz_2 as its Wiener process. We further assume that there is a correlation between the Wiener processes, dz_v and dz_2, which is denoted by σ_{v2} since V_1 and V_2 are correlated. By paying M in marketing costs, a firm effectively purchases the option to exchange V_2 for V_1. M is the cost of this option. Suppose V_1 and V_2 are lognormally distributed, then:

$$\text{Variance}\left(\frac{d[(V_2 / V_1)] / (V_2 / V_1)}{dt}\right) = \sigma^2_v + \sigma^2_2 - 2\sigma_{v2}\sigma_v\sigma_2 = \rho^2 \quad (16)$$

where ρ^2 measures the total uncertainty underlying this subsequent marketing investment. The option to exchange V_2 for V_1, when exercised at some specific maturity date t_2 will yield $V_2 - V_1$, and zero if unexercised. This exchange option is equivalent to a call option on an asset of value V_2 with a strike price V_1. The exercise decision implies that

$$M(V_2, V_1, \rho, t_2) = max[V_2 - V_1, \ 0] \quad (17)$$

where M is the intrinsic value of the call. When adjustments are made to the standard Black-Scholes pricing formula the value of the exchange call option can be expressed as:

$$G_M = V_2 N(d_3) - V_1 N(d_4) \quad (18)$$

where $d_3 = \dfrac{\ln\left(\dfrac{V_2}{V_1}\right) + \rho(t_2 - t)}{\rho\sqrt{(t_2 - t)}}$

and $d_4 = d_3 - \rho\sqrt{(t_2 - t)}$.

2.4 Overall Value of Corporate Growth Opportunities

In sum, the market value of the growth opportunity G_H, due to a successful R&D investment is the real growth option value G_X plus an exchange option on this growth value G_M, pertaining to additional investments in advertising and marketing. That is, for firm H,

$$G_H = G_X + G_M e^{-rt_2}$$

$$= \frac{f(X_H)}{f(X_L) + f(X_H) + r} \left\{ V_1 N(d_1) - K(0)N(d_2)e^{-t(\alpha_h - \alpha_k)} \right\}$$

$$+ e^{-rt_2} \left[V_2 N(d_3) - V_1 N(d_4) \right] \tag{19}$$

2.5 CONCLUSION

We have developed a real options model for valuing growth opportunities of a firm in a competitive environment. The typical firm modeled here is a start-up enterprise that sets to introduce a new product into the market if it succeeds in winning the race to innovate. We assume away any existing assets. The value of the underlying asset, the exercise price and the expiration date of the real call option are considered stochastic.

The underlying asset is the value of a completed R&D project. The maturity date is represented by the date of discovery. The exercise price is the required manufacturing investments once the innovation is successfully made. Volatility of the option comes from the uncertainty of when to innovate, the risk of the project, and the uncertainty surrounding capital expenditures. Capital constraint is implied in the ability to finance competitive R&D. Marketing, which enhances the value of growth opportunities, is incorporated as an exchange real option.

NOTES

1. See *Fortune*, May 24, 1999, "How to be a great eCEO," pages 104–110.

2. See Schmitt (1985) for a good explanation of the difference between basic and applied R&D.

3. Under U.S law, a patent is granted to the person who can prove he or she had the idea first, no matter when he or she filed for the patent. And patent applications remain secret until the patent is granted, a process that

takes 18 months on average but can take more years. Patent owners in the U.S. get a 17-year monopoly on inventions but must share their work with the public. This is a "first-to-invent" standard. Europe and Japan make patent applications public 18 months after they are filed. This is a "first-to-file" standard. The inventor in the U.S. may be tempted to license the patent or take his/her time developing a product, knowing the system will support him/her later. Advocates of the U.S. standard claim the system aims to strike a balance between innovation and competition. But the "first-to-file" system spurs innovators to file for patents faster, speeding the progression from idea to finished product. Critics add that American companies are at a disadvantage because their patent applications languish while technology described in the application is copied or improved upon (See the discussion in *Business Week*, December 2, 1991, page 110). By the time we went to press, it was reported that the U.S. is likely to move toward the European system of administering patent applications.

4. Venture capital angels may demand to have a "feeling" of the potential level of p before agreeing to finance a venture. Recently, they have demanded more unique ideas, and have hired experts in key technology-based industries to command greater scrutiny to the deals. Separately, in 1982 a panel of OECD experts recommended that countries should be asked to list their research facilities which do R&D in biotechnology, indicating the type of research carried out, and the number of personnel and funds involved (Bull, et al, 1982). Granted that, and if research findings were published, and strains and vectors relating to published works were made available to an independent party of scientists, an estimate of p would be possible.

5. See *Business Week*, June 27, 1994.

6. See Kamien and Schwartz (1972), Loury (1979), Lee and Wilde (1980), and Dasgupta and Stiglitz (1980).

7. This approach is similar to Fischer (1978) and Pindyck (1993).

8. We could model $N - 1$ similar firms competing with firm i, without loss of generalities. From firm i's perspective, all the $N - 1$ firms would be low-type, if it were a high-type.

9. This is analogous to the aspect of "technical uncertainty" of Pindyck (1993) and the "idiosyncratic risk" of the R&D model of Berk, et al (1998).

10. Pindyck's (1993) and Berk et al's (1998) single-firm models allude to this as "cost uncertainty" and "systematic risk", respectively. If there were $N - 1$ similar firms competing with firm i, we could express, from firm i's perspective, $\tau_H(X_L) = \min [\tau_j(X_j)]$ of the $N - 1$ rivals; where $j = 1, \ldots, L, \ldots, N - 1; j \neq i = H$.

11. Our model contrasts with the models of Roberts and Weitzman (1981), Weitzman, Newey and Rabin (1981), and Pindyck (1993), which are essentially timeless in the sense that consideration of optimal timing, speed of development, and inter-firm effects are suppressed.

12. See Myers (1977) for a model description of V_1. V_1, the present value of future net cash flows, is adjusted upward or downward as information with strategic impact arrives. Following Myers, we can express V_1 as:

$$V_1 = V_1(X_i, X_j, \sigma, t, s) = \int_t^\infty \left[e^{-rt} \int_0^t q(s)\{V_1(X_i, X_j, \sigma, t, s\}ds \right] dt$$

where: s = State of nature;
   σ = Volatility of the underlying cash flows of the completed R&D project;
   X_i = Firm's R&D;
   X_j = Rival's R&D;
   t = Expiration date.

13. Other studies, for instance, Myers (1977), Majd and Pindyck (1987) and Chung and Charoenwang (1991) model a project value as following a stochastic process while assuming the total required investment and the time the cost is made are known. Broyles and Cooper (1981) also price growth opportunities as a call option but arbitrarily set the asset value, the investment components, and the maturity date.

14. On October 8, 1998 as the Asian financial crisis entered its second year, *The Wall Street Journal* reported that Micron Technology Inc., maker of computer memory chips, together with Idaho congressional delegation, lobbied the U.S. Treasury strongly to require that IMF funds (often below market rate) not be spent to benefit Micron's rivals in South Korea. Separately, Weitzman, Newey and Rabin (1981) and Pindyck (1993), examining infrastructure projects in the U.S., document that unexpected increases in expenditure may lead to termination of otherwise worthwhile capital projects.

15. Majd and Pindyck (1987), Broyles and Cooper (1981), Chung and Charoenwang (1991), and Kester (1984, 1986) assume the exercise price of a real growth option is constant. McDonald and Siegel (1986) and Pindyck (1993) assume the exercise price varies at an assumed rate.

16. Here, we adopt with modifications, the valuation approach of Margrabe (1978) and Carr (1988) that price the options to exchange one risky asset for another.

CHAPTER 3
Comparative Static Analysis

"Breezing through product cycles in one-third of the time that competitors take will earn profits three times as fast and triple growth."
–Authur Andersen & Company[1].

3.1 Introduction

We conduct comparative static analysis to determine how an infinitesimal change in one variable affects the other. In particular, we examine the effect of each relevant parameter on the value of G_X when we differentiate Equation 15 partially with respect to a given parameter. Throughout, G_X is taken to represent the value of growth opportunities or the market value of firm H. The purpose of the exercise is to determine the direction of the relationships between variables as implied by the theoretical model developed in Chapter 2. Later in Chapter 6, we will again put the model to the test and evaluate its performance when subjected to real world data.

3.2 Choice of Level of R&D

As we showed in Equation 14, the objective function of the R&D firm is given as:

$$Maximize \frac{V(t)f(X_H) - X_H}{\left[f(X_H) + f(X_L) + r\right]}. \qquad (14)$$

The first order condition with respect to X_H, taking $f(X_L)$ as given, becomes

$$f(V(t)) + \frac{f'(X_H)}{f(X_L)+r} - \frac{f(X_H)+f(X_L)+r}{f(X_L)+r} = 0 \qquad (14')$$

and the second order condition is

$$f(V(t)) - 2f(V(t)) - \frac{2f'(X_H)}{f(X_L)+r} + \frac{3f'(X_H)[(X_H)+f(X_L)+r]}{f(X_L)+r} < 0 \qquad (14'')$$

where f' and f'' are the first and second derivatives of $f(X)$ with respect to X, respectively.

Suppose $X = X^*$ is the solution for equation 14, X^* would then be the level of R&D investment that guarantees the optimal net benefits. Equation 14, therefore, defines X^* as a function of X_L, N, r and V. We will denote this as $X^* = X^*(X_L, N, r, V)$. From Equations 14' and 14'', we have

$$X_H{}^* = \frac{f(X_H)+f(X_L)+r}{f(X_L)+r} - f(X_H)V[f(X_L)+r] \qquad (16)$$

Suppose we make a Cournot assumption, that each firm expects no reaction from the other competitors in response to a change in its investment strategy. If their expectations are all rational then Equation 16 provides Cournot-Nash equilibrium of R&D investment. We differentiate Equation 16 totally with respect to $f(X_L)$ to obtain:

$$\frac{dX_H{}^*}{df(X_L)} = \frac{1+f'(X_H)}{f(X_H)} - \frac{f''(X_H)[f(X_H)+f(X_L)+r]}{f(X_H)} -$$

$$f(X_H)V - f'(X_H)V[f(X_L)+r] > 0,$$

implying that as competition increases the firm will be inclined to spend more on R&D.

Also,

$$\frac{dX_H{}^*}{dV} = \frac{f'(X_H) - f''(X_H)[f(X_H)+f(X_L)+r]}{f(X_H)} -$$

$$f(X_H)[f(X_L)+r] - f'(X_H)V[f(X_L)+r] > 0,$$

indicating that the larger the value of the potential benefit, the higher the investments in R&D that a particular firm will attract.

3.3 Growth Value in the Case of a Monopoly

Consider a monopolist making R&D investment X, in order to receive benefit V_m at time t when the R&D is successful. Barriers to entry protect the monopolist and the probability that it would make the innovation by that time is $1-e^{-f(X)t}$. Thus it would seek to maximize the present value of the expected net benefit from the discovery. We express this objective as:

$$\text{Maximize}\ \frac{V_m f(X) - X}{f(X) + r}. \tag{17}$$

The solution for Equation 17 requires that the first and second order conditions be satisfied which are, respectively:

$$X = \frac{[f(X) + r] - rV_m f'(X)}{f'(X)} \tag{17'}$$

$$\text{and}\ rV_m f''(X) + Xf''(X) < 0. \tag{17''}$$

It would be of interest to know if a firm's R&D investment is influenced by differences in market structures. We extend this discussion in the next section.

3.4 Growth Value in the Case of Collusion

Suppose these N firms now collude to undertake the R&D investment. Under the terms of the cooperation they will share the receipts of total benefits from the innovation so long as any one of them succeeds by time t. This would occur with a probability density function of $[f(X_H) + \Sigma f(X_L)]e^{-r[f(X_H)+f(X_L)]}$. Let $[f(X_H) + \Sigma f(X_L)] = [f(X_H) + (N-1)f(X_L)] = Nf(X)$, assuming the existence of Cournot-Nash equilibrium. Therefore, the objective of the firm in this case is to maximize total expected net benefit with respect to X and N:

$$\text{Maximize}\ \frac{V_c Nf(X) - NX}{Nf(X) + r} \tag{18}$$

The necessary conditions for X to be a solution are

$$X = \frac{[Nf(X) + r] - rV_c f'(X)}{Nf'(X)} \tag{18'}$$

and $rV_c f''(X) + NXf''(X) < (. \tag{18''}$

Also, for N to be a solution to Equation 18 requires the following first and second order conditions:

$$N = \frac{rV_c f(X) + X[f(X) - r]}{Xf(X)} \tag{19}$$

and $- Xf(X) < 0. \tag{19'}$

Equation 19 gives some interesting results. More firms are attracted to join a cartel the larger the value of expected growth option $[dN/dV > 0]$. Furthermore, suppose N is continuous, it can be shown that as N increases the R&D expenditure of each firm declines $[dN/dX < 0]$. However, there is an optimal size of the cartel if the participating companies maximize total net benefit (see Figure 4.4 in chapter 4).

By examining equations 16, 17' and 18 we find firms pursue different R&D investment strategies under different market structures. Suppose $V=V_m$, Equations 16 and 17' imply that a rival competitive firm invests more in R&D than a monopolist especially if $f(X) < 1/V$. It would seem that factors on which V depends influence the over-investment or under-investment of a rival firm in R&D. For example, a higher strike price will result in over-investment in a comparable project since the option value is lower. Alternatively, if optimal R&D investments are equal, then $V < V_m$. The implication is that a firm under rivalry would need to spend more in R&D in order to be able to reap sufficient potential benefits to match a monopolist.

We also note that the expected benefit a successful firm receives under collusion is larger than that under rivalry [see Equations 16 and 18']. Again, this depends on the parameter values. A firm is attracted to enter a collusive agreement especially if

$$\left[Xf'(X) + f(X)\right] > \frac{r\left[\sum f(X) + r\right]}{\sum f(X)}.$$

On the other hand, if $V = V_c = V_m$, there would always be an overinvestment under competitive rivalry. Given equal net research and development investments, the expected benefits accruing to a monopolist is often larger than those due to collusion or perfect competition ($V < V_c < V_m$).

3.5 Value of Growth Opportunities with R&D

Without considering the exchange component, the growth value is given by Equation 15. That is,

$$G_X = \frac{f(X_H)}{f(X_L) + f(X_H) + r}\left\{V_1 N(d_1) - K(0)N(d_2)e^{-t(\alpha_h - \alpha_k)}\right\}. \text{ Thus,}$$

$$\frac{dG_X}{dX_H} = \frac{f(X_L)f'(X_H) + rf'(X_H)}{\left[f(X_L) + f(X_H) + r\right]^2}\left\{VN(d_1) - K(0)N(d_2)e^{-t(\alpha_h - \alpha_k)}\right\} > 0,$$

implying that a firm's R&D (or IVA) contributes positively to its growth opportunities, holding other factors constant.

3.6 Value of Growth Opportunities with Rival R&D

The derivative of G_X with respect to rival IVA (X_L) is expressed as follows:

$$\frac{dG_X}{dX_L} = \frac{-f(X_H)f'(X_L)}{\left[f(X_L) + f(X_H) + r\right]^2}\left\{VN(d_1) - K(0)N(d_2)e^{-t(\alpha_h - \alpha_k)}\right\} < 0,$$

meaning, larger investments in R&D of rivals have a negative impact on a firm's value.

3.7 Growth Opportunities with Size of Innovation Rents

Given the expression of d_1 and d_2 in Equation 11, the derivative of G_X with respect to V_1 is:

$$\frac{dG_X}{dV_1} = [\frac{f(X_H)}{f(X_L) + f(X_H) + r}]*$$

$$[N(d_1)N'(d_1) - N'(d_2)\{K(0)N(d_2)e^{-t(\alpha_h - \alpha_k)}\}] > 0,$$

since as $V_1 \to \infty$, $d_1 = d_2 = +\infty$ and $N(+\infty) = 1$. $N'(d_1)$ and $N'(d_2)$ are derivatives. Thus, the larger the monopoly rent to be derived from a successful innovation, the greater the size of growth opportunities.

3.8 Growth Opportunities with Strike Price

The derivative of G_X with respect to K is:

$$\frac{dG_X}{dK} = [\frac{f(X_H)}{f(X_L) + f(X_H) + r}]*$$

$$[-N'(d_1) - N(d_2)(-)N'(d_2)\{K(0)N(d_2)e^{-t(\alpha_h - \alpha_k)}\}] = 0,$$

since if $K \to \infty$, then ln $(V/K) \to -\infty$, and $d_1 = d_2 = 0$. It implies that increasing level of strike price (capital expenditure), other factors held constant, erodes the value of growth opportunities. At very large levels of K the value of the real growth option becomes worthless.

3.9 The Impact of R&D on the Expected Time of Discovery

The effect of the incremental change in R&D investment on the expected time of successful completion of the R&D project is derived as:

$$\frac{dt}{dX_H} = \frac{f'(X_H)[f(X_L) - f(X_H)]}{[f(X_L) + f(X_H)]^3} < 0 \text{ if } f(X_H) > f(X_L).$$

That is, increasing levels of R&D lowers the expected time of innovation if a firm's success rate is higher than that of the rival's. So, it pays for a superior firm to spend more money in a targeted R&D investment because that would generate a faster discovery.

3.10 Growth Opportunities and the Expected Time of Innovation

The derivative of G_X with respect to t, the maturity date for the real growth option, is the following:

$$\frac{dG_X}{dt} = \left(\frac{1}{2}\right)\left[\frac{f(X_H)}{f(X_L) + f(X_H) + r}\right]*$$

$$\begin{bmatrix} VN(d_1)N'(d_1)\dfrac{\alpha_h - \alpha_k + \dfrac{\sigma^2}{2}}{\sigma\sqrt{t}} + \\[4mm] N(d_2)N'(d_2)(\alpha_h - \alpha_k)K^{-t(\alpha_h-\alpha_k)}\left(\dfrac{\alpha_h - \alpha_k + \dfrac{\sigma^2}{2}}{\sigma\sqrt{t}} - \dfrac{\sigma}{\sqrt{t}}\right) \end{bmatrix} = 0,$$

as $t\rightarrow+\infty$. Therefore, as time of discovery drags further into the future, the value of growth opportunities vanishes. The longer it takes to make a discovery the higher the likelihood that the benefit of any ultimate innovation will be lost. This may be because competing substitutes are introduced into the market, or the society no longer needs the product. For instance, in the era of high technology, computer software sometimes may have a lifetime of just under one-year.

3.11 Growth Opportunities with Return on Hedge Portfolio

The derivative of G_X with respect to α_h is given as follows:

$$\frac{dG}{d\alpha_h} = \left[\frac{f(X_H)}{f(X_L) + f(X_H) + r}\right]$$

$$[tV_1N'(d_1) + (\alpha_h - \alpha_k)t(\sigma\sqrt{t})^{-1}N'(d_2)*\{K(0)N(d_2)e^{-t(\alpha_h-\alpha_k)}\}]>0,$$

since $d_1 = d_2 = +\infty$, as $\alpha_h\rightarrow+\infty$ and $N'_1=N'_2 = 1$. Thus, the value of the growth option increases with the cost of hedging against the volatility in the strike price.

3.12 CONCLUSION

This chapter has explored the relationships between the key parameters in the real option valuation model. R&D investments by the firm contribute positively to its value of growth opportunities, whereas R&D of the rivals have a negative impact. The longer it takes to exercise the real call option as well as increasing magnitudes of the strike price erode the value of the option. R&D impact the speed of innovation positively. The riskier the project and the higher it costs to hedge volatility in the strike price, the higher the value of growth opportunities.

Other things constant, larger amounts of the potential benefits of innovation draw higher investments in R&D. More firms are attracted to collaborate in R&D only if the expected market potential of the future product is large. However, whereas the R&D cost per firm in a cartel declines, the benefit per firm actually falls faster. On the whole, a monopolist firm invests less in R&D than a firm under competition.

NOTE

1.   Authur Andersen's "rule-of-thumb" as quoted in *Business Week,* October 25, 1991.

CHAPTER 4

Scenario Analysis: A Case Study of a Biotechnology Company

"When we sell a pill, the value of what we sell isn't the chemicals that go into the pill, but the intellectual property that goes into making it."
–Randall Tobias, Eli Lilly & Company[1].

4.1 Company Background

In the fall of 1995, John Anderson and Jane Madigan launched Othogen Incorporated[2], a New York biotechnology start-up firm. The name Othogen will soon become synonymous with weight-loss if the company succeeds in obtaining a patent on its unique gene-splicing technique that has the potential to deliver a cure for obesity. It would revolutionize an industry that is in urgent need for a safe cure but has patients now skeptical of all claims by companies making obesity drugs because of ineffectiveness and worries of side effects. In September 1997, American Home Products Corporation made a surprise recall of Redux and Fenfluramine, two leading drugs in that market, because of new evidence showing they are linked to serious heart-valve problems[3].

Othogen's dream is to identify genetic markers for obesity by splicing genes from affected people into bacteria and studying the strands of DNA (deoxyribonucleic acid) that these patients have uniquely in common[4]. The approach is to identify defective genes and match them with their specific functions in the cell. The bad genes are believed to set on a type of enzyme, which inhibits the function of serotonin, a chemical substance that causes muscles contraction and whose deficiency affects mental activity. So the challenge is not only to slow down the enzyme but to switch off the genes that set the enzyme to work. Because defective genes simply can't be snipped out, Othogen's technique will deactivate them by inserting copies of the genes made in reverse.

Othogen Inc. is among a growing list of firms that believe identifying human genes will provide important new leads to medicines against a wide range of diseases that continue to defy adequate treatment. John Anderson, a renowned research neurologist, left academia to seize the opportunity. He adds that at this point in his career, he is interested in finding "cures," not just causes of diseases, and "only companies do that, not universities." John has teamed up with Jane Madigan, a former graduate student who has been with Spectra Biomedical Inc., a Menlo Park, California company until Glaxo Wellcome PLC acquired the firm.

4.2 Market Trend

According to a report in the Journal of the American Medical Association[5], some 58 million people in the U.S. weigh at least 20% more than their ideal body weight- making them, in the terminology of dietary science, obese. The report shows that the percentage of teens who are overweight, which held steady at about 15% through the 1970s, rose to 21% by 1991. Despite a plethora of diet and fitness programs since the 1980s, Americans have actually put on more weight that they have lost. The average weight gain between the ages 30 and 39 is 4 pounds for men and 9 pounds for women. Of the estimated 80 million Americans who go on a diet each year, 95% gain it back within five years.

Results from a long-term study conducted by the Center for Disease Control (CDC)[6] show that the number of Americans who are seriously overweight, after holding steady for 20 years at about a quarter of the population, jumped to one-third in the 1980s, an increase of more than 30%. A survey across the country indicates there are deep pockets of obesity, especially in rural areas and among certain racial and ethnic groups. The CDC study found that the prevalence of obesity was nearly 50% for black and Mexican-American women - compared with 33.5% for white women. In some Native American communities, up to 70% of adults are dangerously overweight.

In all gender, income and racial groups, genetic factors seem to play a role. Scientists now know that body weight control is linked to the function of the brain, which regulates the rate of metabolism. However, what has never been determined was how that process is biologically triggered and if the elements that create it could be identified, isolated and blocked. The discovery of defective genes responsible for obesity and the technique to switch them off for good will revolutionize the industry. Othogen believes they will not just control the disease but conquer it.

It is estimated that the overweight industry is about $80 billion a year. Othogen plans to initially target the seriously obese patients. This is an $800 million niche. The company hopes the technique will eventually catch on to include people under 20% overweight, or even those who desire cosmetic weight loss. And the possibility of opening up the global market appears to have great potential.

4.3 Industry Competition

Othogen faces stiff competition in the industry. The Food and Drug Administration (FDA) in November approved Meridia, which acts on the brain to produce a feeling of fullness. Knoll Pharmaceutical Company, a unit of Germany's BASF AG, makes the obesity drug that could hit the market sometime in the year 2000. However, besides its less dramatic weight loss effects, the drug has some side effects including dry mouth, constipation, high blood pressure, headache and insomnia.

American Home Products Corporation in September withdrew Redux and Fenfluramine from the market after the FDA determined that patients who were on these obesity drugs had developed primary pulmonary hypertension, a rare lung disease. Like Meridia, Redux and Fenfluramine act to boost the level of serotonin chemical in the brain in order to curb the appetite by helping a person feel full and satisfied.

Still, more competition could come soon from Roche Holding Ltd. The company recently resubmitted its application for approval of its widely awaited obesity drug Xenical, whose clearance had been delayed because of breast-cancer concerns. Experts say Xenical works by a different mechanism and, if approved, could be used in combination with Meridia.

Othogen is confident that their work would be the first of its kind to really introduce a cure for the disease. The firm says the approach of all other obesity drug companies has been to view obesity as a chronic disease, much like high blood pressure, that requires life-long therapy. Moreover, the products of these companies deliver short-lived results and their effects on brain chemicals are apt to produce harmful side effects. Othogen's gene technology would essentially get rid of the defective genes and enhance good ones, freeing the body of any side effects. In addition, no patient with a history of any serious complications like stroke, coronary artery disease, congestive heart failure or uncontrolled hypertension would be excluded from this treatment.

There is a tough competition to face, nevertheless. Many research laboratories in academia, pharmaceutical and biotechnology companies are increasingly using gene-hunting technology as a way of looking for drugs. Thanks to the Human Genome Initiative, an international project partly funded by the U.S. government to map the nearly 100,000 genes found on human chromosomes. The project hopes that by the year 2010 the structure and function of almost all human genes will be understood.

And there is Eli Lilly & Company, the architect of Prozac, the world's leading antidepressant. There is word that Eli Lilly that has been in the forefront of research on central-nervous-system (CNS) receptors is looking for appetite suppression drugs, now that the patent protecting Prozac is expiring in two years. Also, Glaxo Wellcome PLC, Pfizer Inc., Du Pont, Ciba-Geigy, General Electric, Upjohn, Dow Chemical, Merck & Co., Genentech and SmithKline Beecham PLC that have bet huge investments in genetic engineering technology are cited as competitors.

Othogen is aware that to capture the market they must win this competitive race to innovate. John and Jane still recall the words of Steve Paul, Eli Lilly's director of research and development. "CNS research is a game of probabilities. If you have a lot going on, the probability of one compound becoming a breakthrough drug is much higher."[7] Othogen strongly believes they are in what they are best at, and have a concept which when adequately and timely financed could be a blockbuster. Competition in their view merely serves to build primary demand.

4.4 Risks

Some industry experts caution that biotech firms are overly futuristic, gambling with investments whose payoffs are elusive. Basic R&D investments are by nature uncertain. It may be truly a game of probability. Othogen is not certain about the time frame of its innovation. It is, at the same time, uncertain about when any of its competitors could be the first in making the discovery.

More expensive equipment and more insidious diseases have driven the average cost of developing a new drug at big pharmaceutical and biotechnology companies to $231 million, more than doubled the inflation-adjusted cost a decade ago[8]. A firm that wants to build leadership position in such highly competitive and risky markets must be ready to develop innovative products and techniques through a painful process, often willing to incur heavy loses along the way.

Othogen also must face the public perception of genetic engineering, or gene transfer. According to a survey conducted by Prof. Thomas Hoban at North Carolina State University, two-thirds of consumers believe they will personally benefit from biotechnology, and almost 75% believe biotechnology will have a positive effect on food quality and nutrition[9]. However, survey respondents seem unwilling to accept gene transfers between plants and animals or between humans and farm animals. This poses a threat to Othogen's plans to use plant genes instead of human genes, which are much more expensive to extract. After all, the company believes, humans can incorporate plant genes and vice versa, because all living organisms read the same genetic language.

Othogen is troubled that it will unfairly get the taint of biotechnology research from groups including religious organizations concerned about the sanctity of life; environmentalists worried about the release of genetically altered organisms; farmers anxious about paying patent royalties for their animals; and animal protectionists concerned about the increased exploitation and suffering of animals. There are significant government regulatory hurdles also to overcome, stemming from the need to assure the public that the products are safe. Each biotech product currently requires an extended regulatory approval period that, unfortunately, does not take into account the time dimension of capital invested.

Product liability cases are another risk area. Richard Mahoney, Chairman & CEO of Monsanto Company recently warned, "wait until start-up companies see what larger companies have been facing for years in tort cases. Monsanto can handle it, we have the staying power to deal with these obstacles and we have had to face them before. But can the many superb science-based start-up companies do it with their funding limitations? May be-may be not."[10]

At one point, Othogen mulled over the idea of teaming up with other firms to carry out this project. The goal of such a collaborative deal would be to defray costs, spread risks and promote the cross-fertilization of ideas. Jane Madigan experienced such an arrangement in the industry before. Bio Chem Pharma of Canada hatched an AIDS therapy, Glaxo Holdings of U.K. shepherded its clinical trial, and Burroughs Wellcome of U.K. did the marketing[11]. However, alliances are not without drawbacks. They are hard to manage. Miscommunication and mistrust often emerge among members. Worse still, indecision about commitment and what to offer to the alliance may develop.

Othogen is aware that in order to survive they must go beyond research and development into production and marketing. They are now ready to see how, given the idea, speed, risk and competition, the payoff stacks up.

4.5 Investment Analysis

4.5.1 Expected Time of Innovation

R&D investment is crucial in impacting the speed at which Othogen or any other firm could win the competitive race to innovate. The conditional probability of success for a monopoly firm is given in Chapter 2 by Equation 4 as $E[\tau(X_H)] = \dfrac{1}{f(X_H)}$, and for a competitive firm by Equation 8 as $E[\tau(X_H)] = \dfrac{f(X_H)}{[f(X_H)+f(X_L)]^2}$. Suppose Othogen's success rate is denoted by $f(X_H)$ and that of a competitor, say Genentech's, is represented by $f(X_L)$, both expressed as percentages. We assume that the expenditures on R&D for each firm is known and every dollar invested is assumed to be equally valuable.

Table 4.1 The Impact of the Probability of Success on the Expected Time of Discovery

f(x)	5	10	15	20	25	30	40	45	50	60	75
E(τ)	20.0	10.0	6.7	5.0	4.0	3.3	2.5	2.2	2.0	1.7	1.3

Note: Othogen as a monopoly firm. *f(x)* denotes its probability of success, and the expected time of Discovery is given as

$$E[\tau(X_{H)}] = \frac{1}{f(X_H)}$$

Table 4.1 and Figure 4.1 show that if Othogen were a monopolist, its expected time to innovate would decline monotonically as the probability to succeed increases. Suppose Othogen now competes with Genentech. The introduction of a competitor drastically lowers the discovery time as indicated in Table 4.2 and Figure 4.2. However, increasing number of firms lowers the expected value per unit of R&D that each firm receives. This phenomenon is illustrated in Figure 4.3, assuming collusion. It appears an improvement in the

Figure 4.1 The Impact of the Success Rate on the Expected Time to Innovate

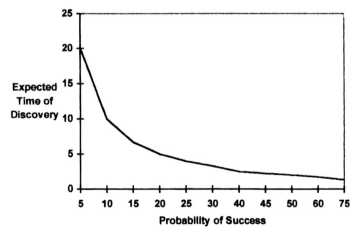

Note: Othogen as a monopoly firm.
Source: Table 4.1.

Table 4.2 The Effect of the Conditional Probability of Success on the Expected Time of Discovery

$f(X_L)$	5	10	15	20	25	30	40	45	50
$f(X_H)$ 5	5.00	2.22	1.25	0.80	0.56	0.41	0.25	0.20	0.17
10	4.44	2.50	1.60	1.11	0.82	0.63	0.40	0.33	0.28
15	3.75	2.40	1.67	1.22	0.94	0.74	0.49	0.42	0.36
20	3.47	2.22	1.63	1.25	0.99	0.80	0.56	0.47	0.41
25	2.78	2.04	1.56	1.23	1.00	0.82	0.59	0.51	0.44
30	2.44	1.88	1.48	1.20	0.98	0.83	0.61	0.53	0.47
40	1.98	1.60	1.32	1.11	0.95	0.82	0.63	0.55	0.49
45	1.80	1.49	1.25	1.07	0.92	0.80	0.62	0.56	0.49
50	1.65	1.39	1.18	1.02	0.89	0.78	0.61	0.55	0.50
60	1.38	1.22	1.07	0.94	0.83	0.74	0.60	0.54	0.49
75	1.17	1.04	0.93	0.83	0.75	0.68	0.57	0.52	0.48

Note: Othogen as a duopoly firm. $E[\tau(X_H)] = \dfrac{f(X_H)}{\left[f(X_H) + f(X_L)\right]^2}$ represents the expected time of discovery. $f(X_H)$ is the conditional probability of success for Othogen, and $f(X_L)$ is the conditional probability of success for Genentech.

success rate for Genentech is also good for Othogen, especially if Othogen has a higher probability. Now consider Genentech at 30% success rate. It is clear that the expected time of innovation first rises as Othogen's probability to succeed goes up, reaching a peak when the rate for Othogen also hits 30%, then it declines thereafter. Does it imply Othogen should settle for a success rate below Genentech's for the sake of achieving a shorter time to innovate? Certainly not if it wants to reap a larger share of the resultant payoff.

4.5.2 Determining R&D Expenditure Levels

The framework for determining the levels of R&D expenditure is based on the investments under collusion where

$$N = \frac{rV_c f(X) + X[f(X) - r]}{Xf(X)}$$

(see Equation 19). We assume away any drawback to the alliance. $f(X)$ represents the instantaneous probability of success for Othogen.

Figure 4.2 The Impact of Competition on the Expected Date of Discovery

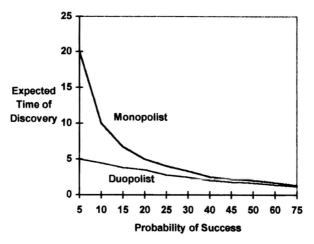

Note: Othogen as a duopolist. The probability of success for Genentech is assumed constant at 5%.
Source: Tables 4.1 and 4.2.

If the collusion is efficient then individual success rates would be indistinguishable, and each firm's probability would equal $f(X)$. V denotes the present value of the cash flows from the completed project, r represents the risk-free rate and N is the number of companies in the cartel. R&D spending is in million of dollars.

Table 4.3 shows that as the number of firms increases, the amount of R&D expenditure per firm declines, other factors held constant. Assume that Othogen is the sole company pursuing this type of project. As observed earlier, in order for the firm to make a faster discovery it must have a high probability of success. Table 4.4 implies that the firm must incur larger amounts of R&D spending to realize this. Also, the risk-free rate, which reflects the cost of capital in the market, is positively related with the size of R&D (Table 4.6). Doubling of the risk-free rate leads to almost double the required amount of R&D. Table 4.5 indicates that R&D increases with both the levels of expected benefits of the project and the success rate.

Table 4.3 Changing R&D Levels with the Number of Competing Firms

N	1	2	4	8	16	32	50	75	100	120
X	120	38.18	16.15	7.5	3.62	1.78	1.13	0.75	0.56	0.47

Note: X is the R&D level, expressed in millions of dollars. N is the number of firms competing in the industry. $N = \dfrac{rVf(X) + X[f(X) - r]}{Xf(X)}$. $f(X) =$ 15%, is the success rate for a firm (for simplicity here assumed equal for all firms). The risk-free rate of interest, $r = 7\%$. And $V = \$800$ million is the project value.

Table 4.4 R&D with Changing Probability of Success

f(X)	2	5	10	15	20	25	30	35	40	50
X	8.62	12.73	15.14	16.15	16.71	17.07	17.32	17.50	17.64	17.83

Note: X is the R&D level, expressed in millions of dollars. $f(X)$ is the conditional probability of success, expressed in percentage. $N = 4$, is the number of firms competing in the industry. $N = \dfrac{rVf(X) + X[f(X) - r]}{Xf(X)}$. $r = 7\%$, is the risk-free rate of interest. And $V = \$800$ million, is the project value.

Table 4.5 Levels of R&D and Project Value with Changing Conditional Probability of Success

	f(X)	5	15	25	35	50	60
V	50	0.795	1.009	1.067	1.094	1.115	1.123
	100	1.591	2.019	2.134	2.187	2.229	2.245
	200	3.783	4.179	4.268	4.375	4.458	4.491
	500	7.955	10.096	10.670	10.937	11.146	11.229
	1000	15.909	20.192	21.341	21.875	22.292	22.459
	1200	19.091	24.230	25.609	26.250	26.751	26.952
	1500	23.863	30.288	32.012	32.812	33.439	33.689

Note: $f(X)$ is the conditional probability of success. $N = 4$, is the number of firms competing in the industry. $N = \dfrac{rVf(X) + X[f(X) - r]}{Xf(X)}$. $r = 7\%$, is the risk-free rate of interest. And $V = \$800$ million, is the project value.

Table 4.6 R&D with Changing Risk-free Rate of Interest

r	5	7	9	11	13	15	17
X	12.00	16.15	20.00	23.57	26.89	30.00	32.90

Note: $f(X) = 15\%$, is the conditional probability of success.

$$N = \frac{rVf(X) + X[f(X) - r]}{Xf(X)}.\ N = 4 \text{ is the number of competing firms.}$$

And $V = \$800$ million is the project value. R&D is in millions of dollars, and r is in percentage.

4.5.3 Computing the Value of Growth Opportunities

Equation 15 is the model for determining the value of growth opportunities (G_x) that Othogen will derive if it succeeds in winning the competitive race to discover a breakthrough cure for obesity. That is,

$$G_X = \frac{f(X_H)}{f(X_L) + f(X_H) + r}\left\{V_1 N(d_1) - K(0)N(d_2)e^{-t(\alpha_h - \alpha_k)}\right\}.$$

Figure 4.3 Intrinsic Value of Growth Opportunities

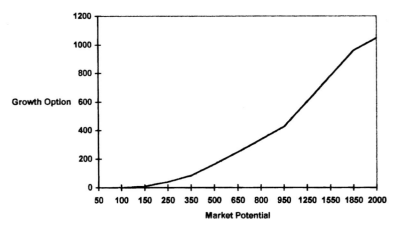

Note: The strike price = $250 million. All other parameters are held constant at values as in table 4.7.

Source: Table 4.7.

Given a market potential value (V_1) of $800 million, it is assumed that the company expects total cost ($K(0)$) of manufacturing, to be $250 million. However, the company strongly feels that the actual cost may change by the time the R&D project is completed. The expected return on this cost structure (α_k) is estimated to be 10% with a standard deviation (σ_k) of 30%. It is possible that Othogen could hedge this uncertainty and the cost of this operation (α_h) is estimated to be 17% annually. The production project is highly correlated ($\sigma_{vk} = 60\%$) with the R&D project. The risk-free rate (r) is 7%.

Othogen is not a diversified entity. Analysts believe, from pure play estimation, it is in the 35% risk (σ_v) class. Industry experts put the company's probability of making a breakthrough discovery at 25%, compared with Genentech's 10%, its only known competitor. Market research estimates a test parameter (∇) of 1.0 is reasonable for this industry sector, given the potential of this company. This parameter accounts for FDA approval period and any clinical trials once the innovation is successful. The market test parameter tends to be higher whenever competing products already exist in the market.

Given all the parameter values, Table 4.7 shows that Othogen would generate growth opportunities (G_X) valued at $349,715,361. Figure 4.4 depicts the call option nature of growth opportunities. It can also be shown that growth opportunities increase with expected return on the hedge security; decrease with expected return on the strike price; increase with volatility of the strike price; and increase with volatility of the R&D project (Table 4.8). However the magnitudes of the impact of these variables on the growth option differ. When growth elasticity constants are computed, the hedge security return is found to have the greatest influence, followed by the expected rate of return on the strike price, volatility of the strike price and volatility of the R&D project.

Suppose Othogen now decides to invest in advertising to open up a larger market. We assume that the expected revenue stream V_2, is highly correlated with V_1, the expected value of the stream of cash flows of the base-case R&D project. The correlation coefficient between V_2 and V_1 is assumed to be $\sigma_{v2} = 80\%$ and they face equal risk ($\sigma_2^2 = 35\%$). The marketing option would be exercised at value date $t_2 = 3.00$. Note that the innovation was patented at value date $t = 2.05$ (see Table 4.7). Suppose the company decides to advertise at t_2, increasing its total expected costs

Table 4.7 Valuation Worksheet

Variable	Notation	Value
Hedge Security Rate of Return	α_h	17.00%
Risk-free Rate of Interest	r	7.00%
Exercise Price Rate of Return	α_k	10.00%
Exercise Price Volatility	σ_k	30.00%
Volatility of Project Value	σ_v	35.00%
Correlation Coefficient (V, K)	σ_{vk}	60.00%
Conditional Variance of R&D Project	σ^2	0.2611
Othogen's Probability of Success	$f(X_H)$	25.00%
Genentech's Probability of Success	$f(X_L)$	10.00%
Expected Expiration Date	$E[\tau(X_H)] = t$	2.0408
Market Test Parameter	∇	1.00
Gross Project Value	V_1	800.00
Expected Exercise Price	$K(0)$	250.00
d_1		2.1540
d_2		1.4239
Cumulative Standard Normal (d_1)		0.9844
Cumulative Standard Normal (d_2)		0.9228
Value of Growth Opportunity	G_X	**349.715**

Note: An analysis of the model specified by growth opportunities,

expressed as $G_X = \dfrac{f(X_H)}{f(X_L)+f(X_H)+r}\left\{V_1 N(d_1) - K(0)N(d_2)e^{-t(\alpha_h-\alpha_k)}\right\}$

The value of the growth opportunities that can be assigned to Othogen is computed using the parameter values explained in the table. d_1 and d_2 are Black-Scholes constants expressed in Equation 12,

$$d_1 = \frac{\ln\dfrac{V}{K(0)} + (\alpha - \alpha + \dfrac{\sigma^2}{2})}{\sigma\sqrt{t}}$$ and $d_2 = d_1 - \sigma\sqrt{t}$. The conditional

volatility of the real option is $\sigma^2 = \sigma_v^2 + \sigma_k^2 - 2\,\sigma_{vk}\sigma_v\sigma_k$. G_X, V and $K(0)$ are in millions of dollars.

from \$250 million to \$300 million in order to help raise the market potential from \$800 million to \$1.2 billion. The value of growth opportunities of Othogen would therefore increase from \$349 million to \$780 million. We demonstrate this valuation in Table 4.9. Table 4.10 presents a summary of the influence of each of the variables on growth opportunities.

Figure 4.4 Effect of Size of Cartel on Growth Value and R&D

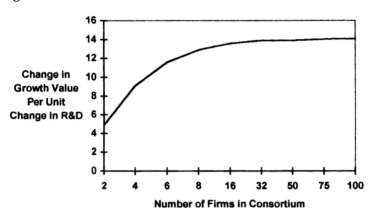

Table 4.8 Effect of Project Volatility on Growth Opportunities

σ_v	5	8	12	15	18	25	30	35	40	45
G	348.4	348.1	348.2	348.3	348.4	348.8	349.2	349.7	350.4	351.1

Note: $G_X = \dfrac{f(X_H)}{f(X_L) + f(X_H) + r}\left\{V_1 N(d_1) - K(0)N(d_2)e^{-t(\alpha_h - \alpha_k)}\right\}$, G_X is in millions of dollars and σ_v, the volatility of the project, is in percentage. All other parameters are held constant at values as in Table 4.7.
Source: Table 4.7.

Table 4.9 Value of Growth Opportunities of Othogen (G_H) with Advertising Expenditure

V_2	1,200	1,800	2,400	3,000	3,600	4,200
$K(0)$	300	350	400	450	500	600
G_X	327	305	284	264	246	213
G_H	757	1,200	1,704	2,215	2,729	3,229

Note: $G_H = G_X + e^{-rt}G_M$. Also, $\sigma_2^2 = 35\%$, $\sigma_{v2} = 80\%$, and $t_2 = 3.00$. We assume that the marketing costs constitute the increase in the level of capital expenditure $K(0)$, from its base value of \$250 million. All values are in millions of dollars. Other parameter values are as in Table 4.7.

Table 4.10 Summary of the Effects of Changes in the Relevant Parameters on Othogen's Growth Opportunities

Variable	Notation	Impact	Comment
Hedge Security Rate of Return	α_h	+	
Risk-free Rate of Interest	r	−	
Exercise Price Rate of Return	α_k	−	
Exercise Price Volatility	σ_k	+	G first falls as σ_k rises but starts to increase at about 10%. But when both σ_k and σ_v rise, G always increases.
Volatility of Project Value	σ_v	+	G declines as σ_v rises but starts to increase at about 14%. But when both σ_k and σ_v rise, G always increases.
Correlation Coefficient (V, K)	σ_{vk}	−	G is highest with perfectly negative σ_{vk}.
Othogen's Probability of Success	$f(X_H)$	+	
Genentech's Probability of Success	$f(X_L)$	−	
Expected Expiration Date	t	−	But $G = 0$ as $t \to +\infty$.
Market Test Parameter	∇	+	
Present Value of Project Cash Flows	V	+	G is worthless at about $V = \$15m$. However, when $V = K = \$250m$, G is still positive at $\$50m$.

Table 4.10 (Continued)

Variable	Notation	Impact	Comment
Expected Exercise Price	$K(\tau)$	–	$G = 0$ as $K(\tau) \to +\infty$, especially when K is more than double V. G is still positive at \$161m even when $V = K = \$800$m.

Note: Growth opportunities,

$$G_X = \frac{f(X_H)}{f(X_L) + f(X_H) + r}\left\{V_1 N(d_1) - K(0)N(d_2)e^{-t(\alpha_h - \alpha_k)}\right\}.$$ As the
level of a variable increases, other factors held constant at values as in table 4.7. G_X may rise (+), fall (–), vanish (0), or remain undetermined (?).

4.6 CONCLUSION

The market value of Othogen Inc., defined as its growth opportunities, is valued as a call option. It is evident that Othogen can boost its probability of succeeding in making a breakthrough discovery by investing more in R&D, the only observable input. Some competition is good for Othogen. It motivates efficient and speedy R&D investments and builds primary demand. As in an option pricing framework, the expected monopoly rent (underlying asset) and its volatility have positive effect on the real growth option. The strike price and its return rate have a negative impact on growth option but its variance has a positive relationship. The return rate on the hedge security has a positive impact. Advertising expenditure enhances the company's growth value.

ACKNOWLEDGEMENT

A major part of this chapter is reprinted from the *Quarterly Review of Economics and Finance,* Volume 38, Special Issue, Richard E. Ottoo, "Valuation of Internal Growth Opportunities: The Case of a Biotechnology Company," pages 615–633, Copyright (1998), with permission from Elsevier Science.

NOTES

1. See *Business Week*, January 11, 1999, page 146.
2. Othogen, Inc. is a hypothetical company.
3. The Wall Street Journal, November 25, 1997, page B1.
4. A gene is the element or unit of a chromosome that carries and transfers an inherited characteristic from parent to offspring and determines the development of some particular character or trait in the offspring. Chromosomes are structures in the cell nucleus containing DNA. DNA is the material of which genes are made.
5. *Time Magazine*, January 16, 1995, pages 58–65.
6. Ibid.
7. Burton, T. M., *The Wall Street Journal*, June 12, 1996.
8. BusinessWeek, July 1, 1991.
9. Genetic Engineering: Opposing Viewpoints, Greenhaven Press, Inc., San Diego, 1996.
10. Bender, David and Bruno Leone, ibid, page 35.
11. See *Business Week*, June 27, 1994.

CHAPTER 5
Financing A Growth Project: A Binomial Approach

"Every new product needs a champion, someone who believes in an idea and is willing to take risks to see that idea grow."
–Business Week.[1]

5.1 Introduction

In general, when a firm elects to undertake an investment opportunity, internal and/or external funds are sought to finance the new activity. Management thus has the option to roll over capital generated by the new enterprise into yet newer ventures within the company at a later date. In a pure Modigliani-Miller world where corporate financing and investment decisions are independent, management can do this without submitting them to the discipline of the capital markets.

However, when a project is conceived and implemented on a stand-alone basis, investment and financing decisions should be made simultaneously due to their important interactions. The typical growth project we have modeled thus far is a fine example of the "stand-alone" nature of an asset. We analyze a simpler scenario where the number of sources of uncertainty is reduced. For instance, the uncertainty with respect to the timing of innovation is suppressed.

In this chapter we examine how valuable investment and financing flexibilities are with respect to undertaking growth

71

opportunities. A brief survey of operating and financing options is also presented. We illustrate a discrete-time valuation analysis with a hypothetical case of a hydroelectric power investment project in an emerging market. In the example, the government is eager to attract and promote private investment. Private investors recognize the growth opportunities available and are willing to participate. However, both sides would wish to know what strategies could be designed to finance this project. We adopt the binomial model, which provides an intuitive and tractable analysis.

Project financing is the financing of a specific economic unit where the cash flows of the project are earmarked as the source of funds from which creditors will be repaid, and where the assets of the project serve as collateral. Assets and cash flows associated with the project are accounted for separately from those of the sponsoring investors or company. Whenever funding for the project is negotiated from external sources creditors have recourse only to the cash flows and assets of the project.

In other words, project financing is an asset-based financing as opposed to a balance sheet financing. It follows, therefore, that as the project continues to operate, its capital is returned to the investors who decide how best it can be reinvested. This suggests that investors, both equity and debt holders will at every stage of the project life-cycle base their financing decisions on the investment outlook of the project. Project financing thus provides investors with the means of carving out value without subjecting it to the exposure of the sponsoring institution or parent company.

5.2 Operating Flexibility

Some researchers have examined the valuation of operating flexibilities in the context of the Options Pricing Theory. McDonald and Siegel (1986) study the optimal timing of investment in an irreversible project where benefits from the project and the investment cost follow continuous time stochastic process. They find that it is optimal to wait until the present value of the benefits is double the investment cost.

Paddock, Siegel and Smith (1988) value the option to wait in an offshore petroleum lease, specifying when and if a firm should explore and develop the tract of land for extracting hydrocarbons. Because the firm can begin development at any time before expiration of the lease, the analogy of the undeveloped reserve is with a stock call option of the American type. The current stock price is represented by the value of developed reserve discounted for development lag; the exercise price is the per unit development cost; the variance of rate of return on the stock is taken to be the variance of rate of change of the value of a developed reserve; time to expiration is the relinquishment requirement which stipulates that the leaseholder must surrender the lease if it does not explore and develop by a certain date; dividend in this case is the net production revenue less depletion; and the riskless rate of interest equally applies.

Trigeorgis (1993) examines a hypothetical oil extraction and refinery project where a large oil company holds a one-year lease to start drilling on undeveloped land with potential oil reserves. The lease allows management to defer investment for up to a year and benefit from resolution of oil price uncertainty during this period. If oil prices increase appreciably, management would invest an amount K. That is, it would exercise its option to extract oil. But if oil prices decline, it would not commit to the project. The firm would reap a value of maximum $[V-K, 0]$ just before expiration of the lease. Trigeorgis finds that the option to defer is analogous to an American call option on the gross present value V, of the completed project's expected operating cash flow, with the exercise price being equal to next period's required outlay. The value of this option would decline with shorter relinquishment requirement, implying early investment sacrifices the option to wait and is justified only if maximum $[V-K, 0]$ is positive.

Kemna (1993) models the option to wait differently by assuming that the exploration time has expired and the Oil Company has to postpone development and thus extend the exploration phase. She further assumes that once the alternative to extend the exploration has been chosen, it is only possible to start development after the expiration of the extended exploration phase. The benefit of exercising the option at the expiration date is the market value of the developed project, and the cost is equal to the investment outlay. Kemna shows that this option is similar to a European call option on an installed project, with maturity date equal to expiration date of the extended license.

Many capital projects usually require many years to develop and complete. Investment decisions and cash outlays occur sequentially. The investment program is thus a contingent claim and becomes productive only after the entire sequence is completed. At every stage, management can choose whether to invest and continue with the project. Such a sequential nature of outlays creates a valuable option to "default" at any instant if, say, the output price drops substantially.[2] The lower the uncertainty, the smaller is the value of this option, since each stage of investment is expected to yield information that reduces the uncertainty over the value of the completed project.

Another valuable option is the opportunity to expand. If market conditions turn out to be more favorable than anticipated, the project can increase the scale of production or step up resource utilization at different times during its life.[3] Suppose management executes a follow-on investment K', which would double the scale and value of the project after one year. The option to expand is thus analogous to a call option to acquire 100% additional part of the base-scale project V', paying K' as exercise price and earning an enhanced value of $\max[2V'-K', V'] = V' + \max[V'-K', 0]$, which is equivalent to the value of the base-scale project plus a call option on future investment. However, if market conditions deteriorate, management will let the option expire unexercised.

On the other hand, the option to contract or scale back can be viewed as a put option on part of the project with a strike price equal to the potential cost savings. If the market is much less favorable than initially expected, management may exercise the option to contract production and forego planned future expenditures.

Should market conditions deteriorate so severely, management might permanently bail out of the project and resell existing assets for value in the secondhand markets. Abandonment of a project can be caused by precipitous fall in consumer demand, creeping resource prices, or unexpectedly unfavorable political and environmental conditions, if there is no obligation to continue despite unprofitable results. Even during construction, if it turns out that current required outlays exceed the value of continuing the project, the project can be abandoned so as to save on subsequent investment outlays.[4] The option to abandon is valued as an American put option on current project value, with an exercise price equal to the resale value of those assets, or the value of assets shifted to a more valuable use. As an analogy with securities put options, this operating flexibility provides insurance against failure.

In practice, it may be advisable for a business to temporarily shut down if operating revenues are not adequate to cover variable costs, until output prices rise sufficiently. This flexibility to operate or shut down in any given period can be seen as a call option to acquire that period's cash revenue by paying the variable costs as the exercise price.[5]

Mason and Merton (1985) and others have also examined "product" flexibility and "process" flexibility in which a firm may alter its choice of output mix and input mix, respectively, in response to a change in relative prices and demand. The stochastic variables here are the prices of competing products and the input costs of competing raw materials. The variable and the switching costs constitute the strike price. This is the option to switch a project possesses to utilize different mixes of inputs to produce the same output, or the same inputs to produce various arrays of outputs. The option to switch use is very valuable in industries where market demands are volatile, and product differentiation and diversity are important. Specific examples are found in automobiles, pharmaceuticals and electronics industries.

Entrepreneurs are sometimes faced with a difficult choice, whether to pursue risky projects that offer a below-target rate of return but could create valuable strategic opportunities later, or to stick with less risky and more immediately profitable ventures. As discussed in Chapter 1, investments like R&D, mergers and acquisitions, roads and railways, lease on undeveloped land may have negative NPV on the basis of their directly measurable cash flows but would still be justifiable because of their potential to open up subsequent new investment opportunities in future. The growth opportunity can be valued as a call options on real assets.[6] The cost of the investment represents the option's exercise price. The value of the option is the present value of expected cash flows plus the value of any new growth opportunities expected. The time to maturity is the time it takes before the opportunity dissipates.

5.3 Financing Flexibility

To capture growth opportunities, however, a project must be financed. Project financing may come through equity or debt. Both equity and debt can be structured in various forms. Just like operating options, a variety of financing instruments also has options embedded in them. Any financial instrument or product designed to fund the growth venture can be priced using real options technique.

Take equity, for example. *Equity* of the project can be viewed as a call option on its total assets. The position of the stockholders is equivalent to a European call option on the value of the project plus a claim to all future dividends. At maturity of debt shareholders have the option to purchase the assets of the project from the bondholders at the face value of the debt.

Additionally, throughout the project's life shareholders may receive dividends. The face value of all outstanding debt will be identical to the exercise price of the call. At any stage, if the value of the project falls below the amount of debt, shareholders will exercise their right to default on debt obligations, handing over the project to the creditors. They can only regain ownership of the project by paying off the debt. In a way, the shareholders have essentially purchased a call option on the value of the project, and the lenders have written this option.

A growth project like ours can also be financed by a procuring a loan commitment. A *loan commitment* is a debt-financing instrument with an embedded option. It is a credit facility which offers a maximum size and maximum period of time over which the borrower can withdraw funds. A loan commitment could be analyzed as a put option sold by the bank.[7] When the commitment rate exceeds the project's spot borrowing rate, the value of the debt exceeds the amount of the loan and the commitment expires unexercised. However, when the commitment interest rate is below the project's borrowing rate, the project exercises the option and sells the debt to the bank.

Suppose a financial intermediary agrees to a term loan but requires a guarantee by the domestic government. A *loan guarantee* can be viewed as an American put option written on the value of the firm. A loan guarantee is like insurance.[8] It will pay any shortfall in the value of the firm necessary to fully repay the debt. At maturity date, if firm value is greater than the debt's promised principal, the guarantor will pay nothing since the firm is sufficiently valuable to retire the debt. However, if the value of the firm is less than the promised principal, the guarantor must pay the difference in order that the debt is fully repaid. A loan guarantee may take several forms, such as tax exemption, output price guarantee, provision of undeveloped land for project site, or securing utilization of established marketing network of a parent company. To raise some capital, the project management may also sell debt with *warrants* attached. A warrant entitles an investor to buy a common share of the enterprise for a fixed price at any time before specified maturity. Note that although warrant holders are not entitled to vote or receive dividends, the exercise price of the warrant is always adjusted for any stock splits or dividend payments. The value of the warrant is proportional to the American call option value on the project.[9]

A *convertible debt* on the other hand allows the bearer to exchange the debt (bond) for a given number of shares of stock any time up to and including the maturity date of the bond. There are many variations of a convertible debt. The issuing firm may also structure it such that when the bearer decides to convert the bonds into a number of shares, according to the specified conversion ratio, the firm would have the option to pay cash equivalent for these shares. This is referred to as the callable and putable feature. A convertible bond is equivalent to a warrant written on the value of the project plus a straight debt with the same coupon rate and maturity as the convertible bond.

5.4 The Project

We consider a hypothetical hydroelectric power project undertaken by an entrepreneurial management team in an emerging market setting. Management secures lease from a government on a dam site to construct a power generation scheme. The project is to be financed by equity E, and a loan commitment L, secured from a consortium of banks.

There are two distinct phases of the project that span over four periods. Phase one is the construction stage, which lasts the entire first period. The second phase is the operating stage, which runs from period two to termination of the project. From the beginning, choice is made for plant capacity to produce at a stepped up rate whenever it turns out that the market demand for electricity is much higher than originally anticipated, thereby providing the option to expand at any appropriate time over the life of the project.

During the construction phase, the project generates no cash flow. However, all investment outlays at construction are assumed covered by the financing package assembled. The production schedule of the plant is known and the electricity produced is sold at a spot price, which fluctuates over time. The value of the project, V, is proportional to the cash flows generated and its movement through time is described by a diffusion-type process:

$$dV = (\alpha V - P)dt + \sigma V dz \qquad (20)$$

where α = the drift rate, the instantaneous expected rate of return to the project per unit time,
σ^2 = the variance of the return on the project per unit time,
dz = a standard Gauss-Wiener process,
P = the total net payments consisting of contractual debt and other outlays.

The market value of the project is assumed to fluctuate stochastically over time, reflecting new information about future cash flows. V is assumed known at $t = 0$, and for our purpose it is taken to be $200 million. Total required investments K_0, also amount to $200 million, leading to a zero NPV project.

All loan principal payments are due in time T when the productive life of the project is also assumed to end. Whenever cash flows are sufficient and project value is in excess of contractually due payments, equity holders may declare a dividend. If the value of the project falls below the amount of total debt, equity holders will choose to default on the payments. Limited liability allows stockholders to abandon the project, handing it over to the creditors.

5.5 The Binomial Framework

We follow the binomial tree method suggested by Cox, Ross and Rubinstein (1979) in representing the movements in the project value. This is undertaken within the principle of risk-neutral valuation which shows the value of a derivative security is independent of the risk preferences of investors. We assume that the process followed by V in a risk-neutral world is a simple two-state fashion, where the life of the option is divided into equal time steps of length $h = t_{i+1} - t_i$. If the project lasts until time T, then the project value must move a total of n steps, such that $nh = T$. We assume a yearly interval, giving $h = 1$. In time h, V moves up (good state) a proportional amount u with risk-neutral probability θ, or down (bad state) by a proportional amount d with risk-neutral probability $(1-\theta)$, where

$u = e^{\sigma\sqrt{h}} - 1$ is the upward change,
$d = e^{-\sigma\sqrt{h}} - 1$ is the downward change,
$\theta = \dfrac{(1 + rf) - d}{u - d}$ represents the risk-neutral probability, and
r_f denotes the risk-less rate of interest.

We assume that a utilities portfolio is traded in the financial market with exactly the same risk characteristics as the project, yielding an expected rate of return of α. The dynamics of the project value, implied in u and d, represent project volatility of σ. We denote the value of V at node (i, j) by V_{ij}, where $i = 0, 1, 2, 3, 4$; $j = 0, 1, 2, 3, 4$. i indicates the number of periods, and j represents the number of up movements covered for the corresponding i. Note that at each node, the sum of the up and down movements must equal the number of periods. Whenever $i = j$, it is an all-good state, all periods. And if $j = 0$, it is an all-bad state, all periods, implying that the states should not outgrow the periods.

The gross value of the project can thus be derived as

$$V_{ij} = u^j d^{l-j} V_{0,0} \qquad (21)$$

For example, at nodes M and N, $V_{1,1} = uV_{0,0}$ and $V_{1,0} = dV_{0,0}$, respectively.

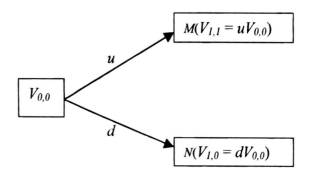

Suppose estimated variable inputs are such that $V_{0,0}$ = $200 million, α = 25%, r_f = 10% and h = 1. Then, u = 1.2840, d = 0.7788, θ = 0.6358 and $(1-\theta)$ = 0.3642. The movement in project values would, therefore, be as shown:

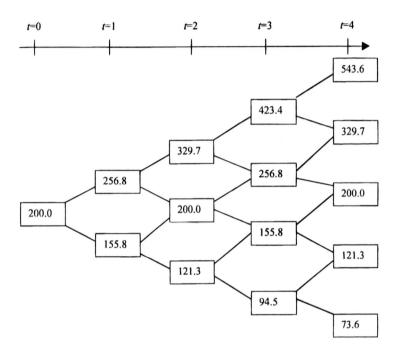

5.5.1 Equity Value

We evaluate equity as a call option on the project value, with the face value of debt as strike price. A call option owner will always only exercise the right to buy if it is deep-in-the-money. That is, if exercising the option is to his or her advantage. If the project value at expiration is less than the face value of debt, exercising the right is not desirable and the option expires worthless, leading to $E_{i,j}$ = 0. However, if the project value is greater than the strike price (out-of-the-money), equity value will be equivalent to that positive difference. At time T, on the debt's maturity date, the value of this call option is known and is expressed as:

$$E_{ij} = \max[V_{ij} - L_i, \quad 0], \text{ for } i = 4; \text{and } j = 0,1,2,3,4; \qquad (22)$$

where L_i, the face value of the loans, is the contractually due payments on the loans at maturity.

By assuming risk neutrality and no possibility of exercise, the equity value at time $T\text{-}h$ is calculated as the expected value of the call option at T, discounted over h. That is,

$$E_{ij} = \left[\theta E_i +_{1j+1} +(1-\theta)E_i +_{1j}\right] / \left(1+r_f\right); \ i = 0,1,2,3; \ j = 0,1,2,3. \quad (23)$$

By recursive method, equity values at all nodes are thus computed at $T\text{-}2h$, $T\text{-}3h$, and $T\text{-}4h$. Suppose the banks agree to give L_0=$100 million but demand a return on their capital of r_d =15%. At maturity, $L_4 - \$100 (1.15)^4 = \$174.9$ million. Hence,

$E_{4,4}$ = max[543.61–174.9, 0] = \$368.71 million,
$E_{4,3}$ = max[329.74–174.9, 0] = \$154.84 million,
$E_{4,2}$ = max[200.00–174.9, 0] = \$25.10 million,
$E_{4,1}$ = max[121.31–174.9, 0] = \$0, and
$E_{4,0}$ = max[73.58–174.9, 0] = \$0.

From Equation 4, and utilizing the values of θ and r_f given above,

$E_{3,3}$ = [$\theta E_{4,4}$+ (1–θ) $E_{4,3}$]/(1 + r_f)
    = [0.6358(368.71) + 0.3642(154.84)]/(1.10) = \$264.38 million.

Similarly,

$E_{3,2}$ = \$97.81 million,
$E_{3,1}$ = \$14.51 million, and
$E_{3,1}$ = \$0.

Rolling back one step further, we obtain

$E_{2,2}$ = [0.6358(264.38) + 0.3642(97.81)]/(1.10) = \$185.20 million,
$E_{2,1}$ = \$61.34 million, and
$E_{2,0}$ = \$8.39 million.

At $t = 1$, $E_{1,1}$ = [0.6358(185.20) + 0.3642(61.34)]/(1.10) = \$127.36 million, and $E_{1,0}$ = \$38.23 million. Thus, equity value at node (0,0) is computed as

$E_{0,0} = [0.6358(127.36) + 0.3642(38.23)]/(1.10) = \$86.27$ million.

As creditors' rates of return on debt change, equity values also change. Essentially, increasing the cost of debt (r_d) represents a growth in the level of the strike price. Table 5.1 shows the results of this change. The higher the exercise price, reflected in the increase in payoff demanded by the debt holders, the lower the value of equity. *Ceteris paribus*, equity with an exercise price of L_i is worth less than equity with an exercise price of L_j, where $L_i > L_j$.

We also examine equity values at different levels of project risk while holding the return rate demanded on debt and other variables constant. The findings presented in Table 5.2 indicate that the more volatile a project the more valuable is an equity holding on it. Increased variance of project return implies higher probability that the future value of the project will be increasing, meaning there is a high probability that the level of payoff to shareholders will be high. Higher volatility may also mean high probability that the future project value will be low. However, downward losses are limited to zero.

Table 5.3 shows equity values at varying risk-free rates. Volatility, debt level, and the return on debt are assumed constant. The higher the risk-free rate of interest, the larger the value of equity. This follows since as interest rates go up, the present value today of the expenditure of the strike price declines.

5.5.2 Debt Value

According to Merton (1974), the value of the risky debt on its maturity date is the minimum of its face value L, and the project value V, and can be expressed as:

$$D_{ij} = \min[V_{ij}, \ L_i], \quad i = 4; \ j = 0,1,2,3,4. \tag{24}$$

Table 5.1 Equity Value with Changing Strike Prices

Cost of Debt (r_d)	10%	15%	20%	25%
Equity Value (E)	103.0	86.3	68.8	55.3

Note: $L_0 = \$100m$, $r_f = 10\%$, $\sigma = 25\%$, $T = 4$ and equity values are in millions of dollars.

Table 5.2 Effect of Project Volatility on Equity Value

Volatility (σ)	10%	15%	20%	25%	30%	35%	40%	45%
Equity (E)	80.6	81.1	83.2	86.3	90.0	94.1	98.5	102.9

Note: $L_0 = \$100m$, $r_f = 10\%$, $r_d = 15\%$, $T = 4$ and equity values are in millions of dollars.

Suppose $r_f = 10\%$, $\sigma = 25\%$, and $r_d = 15\%$, then $L_4 = \$100(1.15)^4$ = \$174.9 million. Subsequently, $D_{4,4} = \min[543.61, 174.9] = \$174.9m$. Similarly, $D_{4,3} = \$174.9m$; $D_{4,2} = \$174.9m$; $D_{4,1} = \$121.31m$ and $D_{4,0} = \$73.6m$. We work recursively, in a similar procedure applied in the previous sub-section, and obtain the value of debt $D_{0,0}$, to be equal to \$113.75 million. Debt values are then computed to determine the effects of project volatility, riskless interest rates, return on debt, and maturity to yield the results shown in Tables 5.4 to 5.7 below.

The higher the rate of return required by the debt holders, the larger the principal payments. Other factors remaining constant, as project volatility rises the value of debt declines. Increasing risk causes debt value to fall because the expected loss to the debt-holders from default of shareholders increases. Also, the higher the risk-free rate, the lower the value of debt. A surprising finding is the effect of maturity on debt value. As presented in Table 5.6, lengthening the maturity of debt increases its value. This contradicts earlier results (see Merton, 1974) which show that longer maturity dates make the present value of the promised principal lower, causing the value of debt to fall.

5.5.3 The Option to Defer Investment

Management may elect to postpone starting up the project for a year to benefit from resolution of uncertainties. We make an

Table 5.3 The Value of Equity at Varying Risk-free Rates of Interest

Risk-free Rate (r_f)	5%	8%	10%	12%	15%
Equity (E)	69.4	79.6	86.3	92.7	102.0

Note: $L_0 = \$100m$, $\sigma = 25\%$, $r_d = 15\%$, $T = 4$ and equity values are in millions of dollars.

Table 5.4 Debt Value and the Cost of Debt

Cost of Debt (r_d)	10%	15%	20%	25%
Debt Value (D)	97.0	113.7	131.2	144.7

Note: $L_0 = \$100m$, $\sigma = 25\%$, $r_f = 10\%$, $V_{0,0} = \$200m$, $T = 4$ and debt values are in millions of dollars.

Table 5.5 The Value of Debt at Different Levels of Project Risk

Volatility (σ)	10%	15%	20%	25%	30%	35%	40%	45%
Debt (D)	119.5	118.9	116.8	113.8	110.0	105.9	101.5	97.1

Note: $L_0 = \$100m$, $r_f = 10\%$, $r_d = 15\%$, $V_{0,0} = \$200m$, $T = 4$ and debt values are in millions of dollars.

Table 5.6 Maturity Date and Debt Value

Maturity (T)	1	2	3	4
Debt (D)	104.6	108.1	112.2	113.7

Note: $L_0 = \$100m$, $r_f = 10\%$, $r_d = 15\%$, $\sigma = 25\%$, $V_{0,0} = \$200m$, and debt values are in millions of dollars.

Table 5.7 The Value of Debt at Varying Risk-free Rates of Interest

Risk-free Rate (r_f)	5%	8%	10%	12%	15%
Debt (D)	130.7	120.4	113.7	107.3	98.0

Note: $L_0 = \$100m$, $r_d = 15\%$, $\sigma = 25\%$, $V_{0,0} = \$200m$, $T = 4$ and debt values are in millions of dollars.

assumption here that the project is wholly equity financed. The option to wait is analogous to a call option on the project value. The exercise price is the investment outlay K_1, that would be made next year at $t = 1$ instead of at $t = 0$ which could have been the case if there were no opportunity to wait. Given that $K_0 = \$200$ million and $r_f = 10\%$, $K_1 = \$200(1.1) 1 = \$220$m. Thus, $E_{1,1} = \max[V_{1,1} - K_1, 0]$ = $\max[256.80 - 220, 0] = \$36.8$ million. With this positive option value, the decision at node (1,1) would be to defer investment. Also, $E_{1,0} = \$0$ leading to an "invest now" decision at node (1,0). Therefore, the enhanced value of the project, which includes the value of the option to defer, is:

$$E_{0,0} = [\theta E_{1,1} + (1 - \theta) E_{1,0}]/(1 + r_f) = \$21.27 \text{ million.}$$

Incorporating the value of flexibility, we know that:

Enhanced NPV = passive NPV + value of embedded option.

Since the passive NPV of this project is zero, the value of the option to defer investment is therefore equal to $21.27 million. As project risk increases, the option to defer investments becomes more valuable. This would mean that merely adopting a project on the basis of its positive NPV while ignoring the impact of its volatility would lead to a substantial loss of value. We present some results in Table 5.8 below.

We also analyze the option to wait under different volatilities and risk-free rates. The riskless rate in this case affects both the strike price and the option value itself. As the risk-free interest rates go up, the present value of the exercise price declines. This leads to a higher value of the option to defer. The results are presented in Table 5.9.

Table 5.8 Value of the Option to Wait (E_w) with Increasing Risk

σ	5%	10%	15%	20%	25%	30%	35%	40%	45%	50%
E_w	0.0	0.6	7.1	14.0	21.3	28.9	36.9	45.3	54.1	63.4

Note: $r_f = 10\%$, $V_{0,0} = \$200$m, $K_{0,0} = \$200$m, $T = 4$ and the values of the option to wait are in millions of dollars.

Table 5.9 Combined Effect of Project Risk and Risk-free Rate on the Value of Option to Wait

Risk-free Rate (r_f)	5%	8%	10%	15%	20%
Volatility (σ) 5%	0.2				
10%	7.6	4.1	0.9		
15%	13.4	11.0	8.9	2.0	
20%	18.8	17.0	15.4	10.3	3.4
25%	23.9	22.5	21.3	17.1	11.7
30%	29.0	27.8	26.8	23.4	18.8
35%	34.0	33.0	32.1	29.2	25.3
40%	38.9	38.0	37.3	34.7	31.4
45%	43.8	43.0	42.3	40.1	37.1
50%	48.5	47.9	47.2	45.2	42.6

Note: $V_{0,0}$ = $200m, $K_{0,0}$ = $200m, T = 4 and the values of the option to wait are in millions of dollars.

5.5.4 *The Option to Abandon Project during Construction: Whole Equity Financing*

Suppose investment outlays will be paid in installments. The first payment of I_0 = $100 million is made immediately, and the remaining $I_1 = (K_0 - I_0)$ = $100m is paid at t = 1, contingent on the outcome that subsequent project value will exceed this amount of expenditure. If the project value is not higher, management will abandon the project and save I_1. The balance of $100 will be kept in an escrow account and will be paid at t = 1 at a level of $100(1 + r_f)$ = $100 (1.10) = $110m. Thus, the value to equity holders with available option to default at construction is given by

$E_{1,1}$ = max[$V_{1,1}$ − I_1, 0] = max[256.80 − 110, 0] = $146.8 million, and
$E_{1,0}$ = max[155.76 − 110, 0] = $45.76 million.

Therefore, the enhanced value of the investment opportunity is

$E_{0,0}$ = [$\theta E_{1,1}$ + (1 − θ) $E_{1,0}$]/(1 + r_f) − I_0 = $0,

such that the value of the option to default equals $0. According to the formulation above, the option to default can also be viewed as a compound call option on the investment opportunity, with the investment installment I_0 as the exercise price.

It is clear from Table 5.10 that the higher the level of the first installment of the investment outlays, the less likely are equity holders willing to walk away from the project. First year investment of at least 30% of total expenditure would generate zero value of the option to default. The default option value increases with a decrease in I_0. If, say, management invests I_0 but the project turns out to be a failure by the end of period one, the losses could be limited to just I_0. In other words, the ability to reduce the downside risk increases with a decrease in I_0.

Consider I_0, spent as a start up cost, is now lent by the banks who demand to be repaid in period two with an equilibrium return rate of r_d. Therefore, the required investment balance I_1 must now be contributed by equity. Management will commit this remaining investment outlays in period one only if project value exceeds the equity cost installment, which equals $I_1 (1 + r_f)$. We compute the value of equity with debt obligation in period two. Suppose the banks give $60 million and only ask for the riskless rate of interest, such that $r_d = r_f = 10\%$. Then $L_2 = \$60(1.10) = \$72.6$ million. Thus,

$E_{2,2} = \max[329.74 - 72.6, 0] = \$257.14$ million,
$E_{2,1} = \max[200.00 - 72.6, 0] = \$127.40$ million,
$E_{2,0} = \max[121.31 - 72.6, 0] = \$48.71$ million, and
$E_{1,1} = [(0.6358)(257.14) + (0.3642)(127.4)]/(1.10) = \$190.81$ million,
$E_{1,0} = [(0.6358)(127.14) + (0.3642)(48.71)]/(1.10) = \$89.77$ million.

Therefore, in valuing total investment including the option of equity holders to default in the presence of debt repayment, we use $E_{2,2}^{\circ} = \$257.14m; E_{2,1}^{\circ} = \$127.40m; E_{2,0}^{\circ} = \$48.71m;$ but

Table 5.10 The Value of the Option to Default (E_d) at Construction: Whole Equity Financing

I_0	100	60	59	58	57	56	55	50	40	20	10
E_d	0	0	0	0.2	0.5	0.9	1.2	3.1	6.7	13.9	17.6

Note: $r_f = 10\%$, $\sigma = 25\%$, $V_{0,0} = \$200m$ and the values of the option to default are in millions of dollars.

$E°_{1,1} = \max[190.81 - 154.0, 0] = \$36.81$ million,
$E°_{1,0} = \max[89.77 - 154.0, 0] = \$0.$

Thus, $E°_{0,0} = \$21.28$ million is the value of the option of equity holders to default under the framework of leverage financing, which is approximately 11% of the project base value. We compute the value of this option at different leverage ratios and cost of debt and present the outcome in Table 5.11. Whenever $r_d = r_f$ the value of the default option is highest, and remains constant until the leverage ratio exceeds 70%. At this point it will tend to rise. In general, the option value declines with increasing leverage and rising cost of debt.

Table 5.11 The Value of the Option of Equity Holders to Default under Leverage Financing

r_d	10%	15%	20%	25%	30%	35%	40%
$I_0 = 40$	21.3	18.9	16.4	13.9	11.2	8.4	5.5
60	21.3	17.7	14.0	10.2	6.2	2.0	0.0
80	21.3	16.6	11.6	6.5	0.0	0.0	0.0
100	21.3	15.4	9.2	2.8	0.0	0.0	0.0
120	21.3	14.2	6.8	0.0	0.0	0.0	0.0
140	21.3	13.0	4.7	0.0	0.0	0.0	0.0
160	21.3	14.0	7.8	1.2	0.0	0.0	0.0
180	21.3	17.9	10.9	3.5	0.0	0.0	0.0

Note: $r_f = 10\%$, $\sigma = 25\%$, $V_{0,0} = \$200m$, $K_0 = \$200$, I_0 and the values of the option to default are in millions of dollars.

5.5.5 The Option to Expand the Project

Management elects to expand the project by 100% of base scale value in period two in response to an expanding demand in the electricity market. To achieve this, additional expenditure of K_2 must be committed. At end of period two the value of this enhanced investment due to the embedded option to expand would be:

$$E_{2,2} = V_{2,2} + \max[V_{2,2} - K_2, 0] = \max[2V_{2,2} - K_2, V_{2,2}] \quad (25)$$

Similar binomial analysis is done at every relevant node. Assuming that $\sigma = 25\%$, $r_f = 10\%$ and $K_2 = \$60$ million, working recursively leads to the value of the option to expand of $350.4 million, about 175% of the value of the base scale project. Table 5.12 shows that as the amount of additional capital investments increases, the option to expand declines in value. Furthermore, it can also be shown that as the time to maturity of the project shortens, the option value goes up.

Table 5.12 The Effect of Additional Outlays on the Value of the Option to Expand (E_x)

K_2	60	80	100	120	140	160	180	200	220	240
E_x	350.4	333.9	317.4	300.8	286.4	272.0	257.7	243.3	236.7	230.0

Note: r_f = 10%, σ = 25%, $V_{0,0}$ = $200m, K_0 = $200, T = 4, K_2 and E_x are in millions of dollars.

5.6 CONCLUSION

Whenever the project is wholly equity financed, equity holders have a higher probability to default during construction the smaller the investment installment cost. Under leveraged financing, the value of the option of equity holders to default decreases. In particular, the option value goes down substantially as debt holders demand a higher return. Thus, the ability to share project risk with the creditors gives the shareholders extra premium to participate in the project. Additionally, increasing leverage means an increasing proportion of risk will be borne by the creditors, causing the value of the option of equity holders to default to drop. However, further increases in leverage in excess of 70% for debt returns of up to 25% increases the value of default option since shareholders find that their diminishing stake in the value of the project is not sufficient to compensate them for the risks being borne.

The option to defer investments becomes more valuable as project risk increases. This would imply that merely adopting a project on the basis of its positive NPV while disregarding the increase in volatility could lead to a substantial loss of value. However, these gains may be eroded by a rising level of interest rates which lower the value of this option since the postponed investment outlays, the exercise price, grows with an increase in interest rates.

The option to expand the project is found to possess significant value, especially if the additional investment outlays required to support this expansion is low. Furthermore, the option to expand is more valuable later than earlier in the life of the project. Unlike debt, equity gets more valuable the higher the risk of the project. Essentially, value additivity of the balance sheet items conforms to the put-call parity condition.

NOTES

1. See *Business Week,* August 16, 1993.
2. Majd and Pindyck (1987) and Trigeorgis (1993) value this time-to-build option, showing that the project is a compound option where each investment buys an option to make the next expenditure.
3. Trigeorgis and Mason (1987) analyze this option.
4. Related studies of the abandonment flexibility include Myers and Majd (1990), Bjerksund and Ekern (1990), and Brealey and Myers (1991).
5. See McDonald and Siegel (1985) and Trigeorgis and Mason (1987).
6. See Myers (1977), Kester (1984), Brealey and Myers (1991) and Trigeorgis (1993).
7. See Thakor, Hong and Greenbaum (1981).
8. See Mason and Merton (1985).
9. Refer to Brealey and Myers (2000) for an excellent discussion on valuing warrants and convertibles "Warrants and Convertibles," Chapter 22.

CHAPTER 6

Empirical Analysis

"With Global lenders going cold on emerging markets, Farmacias
Benavides SA is likely to have to rely on internal
resources to fund future expansion"
–Jaime Benavides Pompa,
Farmacias Benavides SA, Mexico[1]

6.1 Data Sources and Empirical Design

6.1.1 Hypothesis

The valuation model presented in Chapter 2 provides the basis for the hypothesis to be tested. The purpose of the empirical tests is to examine the impact and relevance of identified variables as determinants of real growth options. Rather than lumping companies together and evaluating their competitive investments in acquiring growth opportunities, we divide the sample into emerging and mature firm groups in order to avoid obscuring important qualitative differences that exist between assets-in-place and intangible real growth options. Emerging companies are expected to have predominantly real options in their market value, as opposed to established firms with relatively more assets-in-place.

We have argued that information asymmetry introduces a capital markets constraint on emerging firms making them more dependent on internal capital as a means of accessing strategic growth opportunities. Access to internally generated funds is thus a binding constraint for emerging firms and not for matures firms.

One should expect growth in assets, the net investment component of internal capital, to have a positive effect on real growth options of an emerging firm more than they would have on a mature firm. Similarly, the number of patents and R&D spending are variables measuring outcomes of the competitive race for basic R&D. We test if they are valuable, and determine how different their impact on the sub-samples are, together with rival R&D. For emerging firms, investments in the real options are expected to exhaust internal cash flows. Thus, operating cash flows should have a negative correlation with growth opportunities.

Option pricing theory tells us that volatility of an underlying asset is positively related to the value of the option written on that asset. We therefore expect volatility of potential benefits of innovation to have a positive effect on growth opportunities. Similarly, innovation rent is expected to have a positive correlation with real growth options. We posit that growth in sales is a good industry indicator of the potential rents to be captured through competitive investments. A measure of industry concentration is also included. However, it is not clear whether a high level of industry concentration signifies available rents.

We hypothesize that due to the nature of the basic R&D investments, capital expenditure is an essential price to pay in order to produce the product and capture the expected benefits resulting from the success of the R&D investments. However, uncertainty of capital requirement levels may be undesirable since it potentially increases the cost of acquiring the benefits and the option value is lowered. A mature company that supposedly has a reservoir of retained earnings and easier access to the capital markets may be better positioned to hedge volatility in capital requirements than an emerging firm.

A number of control variables are incorporated in the analysis. It is conceivable that an old company may capitalize on its long presence in a market, rather than an emphasis on idea generation and new concept building, to compete for potential benefits. Age of a company is included to control for such influences plus the possible effects of "first-mover premium." We also include a measure for labor capital to account for contributions to growth due to labor productivity.

Growth opportunities, G_t, is related to a number of relevant parameters (see Equation 15) and is represented as a function:

$$G_t = G_t(V, P, K, X, Y, \sigma_v, \sigma_k, \alpha, D, CF, ET, HH, L), \qquad (26)$$

where V represents the expected monopoly rents to be derived once the R&D is successful and the manufacturing investments are in place; P denotes the relative probability of innovation of firm i; K stands for the level of capital expenditures of the firm; X denotes the firm's R&D investment; Y is the rival firms' R&D; σ_v and σ_k represent the volatilities of the project value and capital expenditures, respectively; α is the second measure of volatility of capital outlays and denotes the premium required to hedge uncertainty in the strike price; D represents the debt-equity ratio; CF is operating cash flows; ET denotes age of the company; HH stands for the Herfindhal-Hirschman index, a measure of industry concentration; and L represents labor productivity.

Cross-sectional regressions, year-by-year and across firms, are conducted to analyze the linear form of the growth function above. We present the results for each year, rather than manipulating time-series averages, in line with Stulz's (1990) suggestion that the distribution of cash flows matters to shareholders period-by-period because shareholders want to optimize resources under managerial control each period to maximize their wealth. The view of Fama (1990) is also that the longest into the future the market can predict is two years.

Besides current values, past and future expected values of these variables are included because we believe they interact in some way in influencing growth opportunities. For example, to investigate the influence of R&D on growth opportunities, we apply all current, past change and future change in R&D as explanatory variables. In a one-year regression, scaled past change in R&D is represented as $\Delta X_{t-1} = (X_t - X_{t-1})/A_t$. Similarly, $\Delta X_{t+1} = (X_{t+1} - X_t)/A_t$ denotes future change in R&D of the firm.

The final form of the least-squares regression equation (not showing stock or change variables) for testing the hypothesis expresses growth opportunities G_t, as the dependent variable:

$$G_t = \gamma + \beta_1 V + \beta_2 P + \beta_3 K + \beta_4 X + \beta_5 Y + \beta_6 \sigma_v + \beta_7 \sigma_k$$

$$+ \beta_8 \alpha + \beta_9 D + \beta_{10} CF + \beta_{11} ET + \beta_{12} HH + \beta_{13} L + \hat{e}_t \qquad (27)$$

where γ is the intercept coefficient of the regression; $\beta_1, \beta_2, \dots \dots$, β_{13}, are the coefficients of the independent variables fully described below; and $\hat{e}_t$ is the error term.

6.1.2 *Overview of Empirical Studies*

Our contribution to the empirical literature stems from the sample construction and the broad scope of empirical methodology used. The sample design into emerging and mature panels enhances a rich observation of the influence of growth opportunities on investment and financing strategies that firms adopt as a result of the qualitative differences between assets-in-place and real growth options in their asset structures. Our methodology is able to examine capital structure and investment decisions of a firm simultaneously, and is able to identify firm characteristics that have not been previously considered. It also enables us distinguish between expenditures on growth opportunities and outlays to maintain assets-in-place. The inclusion of a set of control variables is unique. For instance, we assume that every unit of R&D expenditure is equally valuable and recognize that research and development process entails learning. However, a company should not be rewarded or penalized in this process because of sheer age. We thus include age as a control variable.

Numerous studies have empirically investigated investment opportunities very restrictively by only looking at the investment variables like R&D; R&D and patents; or advertising and R&D. Others have exclusively explored financing and the effects of risk; risk and market structure; and capital expenditures.[2]

Our sample covers seven industries in contrast with other studies, which are industry-specific.[3] Industry-specific empirical analyses tend to miss the cross-sectional variation in some firm characteristics that are predicted to be associated with growth opportunities.

Several authors have applied the event-studies methodology, which have become standard in finance literature in testing financing, investment and operating decisions on the returns of a firm.[4] As pointed out by Fama and French (1997), the periods surrounding the announcements of identifiable events in event-studies tend to be short. Thus, the value effects measured by testing for abnormal stock returns may be small and less reliable. We apply their cross-sectional methodology which may be more informative since it examines cumulative effects of longer-term (one and two years) valuation.

6.1.3 *Description of Variables*

The relative excess value procedures of measuring capitalized market value is employed to proxy the value of growth opportunities.

The market value of the firm (*MV*) is composed of the value of assets already in place (*A*) and the present value of growth opportunities (G_t). The relative excess value of the firm is thus measured as the market value of common plus the book value of debt (*MV*) minus the book value of assets (*A*) normalized by assets (*A*). We compute the market value of common as closing stock price times the number of shares outstanding. In our regression equation, normalized growth opportunities $\left(\dfrac{G_t}{A}\right)$, is the dependent variable. In the event that data points for computing replacement costs are very limited, especially for emerging firms, we believe that $\left(\dfrac{G_t}{A}\right)$ proxies average Tobin's Q reasonably well by using book assets as a proxy for replacement costs. Tobin's Q has been widely applied in finance literature.

Industry is defined by the two-digit Standard Industrial Classification (SIC) code. All variables are normalized by total assets unless otherwise specified. The description of the explanatory variables follows:

V: represents the expected innovation (monopoly) rents and is proxied by two variables. One is the growth rate of sales derived by applying a simple exponential trend regression of net sales. In the year-by-year cross-sectional regression, we instead use expected change to represent growth rate of sales. For example, the expected change (value) in sales over the next one year is expressed as $\dfrac{Sale_2 - Sale_1}{Asset_1}$. The other variable is the Herfindhal-Hirschman index (*HH*) calculated by expressing market share of each firm (using sales) in the industry as a percentage, squaring these figures, and summing them up.

P: denotes the relative probability of innovation and is proxied by the number of patents divided by the industry number of patents. We also include *PP,* the stock of patents obtained by dividing cumulative patents within the past 17 years by industry stock of patents.[5] Both *P* and *PP* are scaled by the ratio of firm assets to industry assets.

K: the strike price is estimated by the levels of capital expenditures.

X: represents current R&D spending.

Y: denotes rival R&D expenditures and is computed as R&D of the industry less R&D of the firm.

σ_v: project volatility, is measured by the Chauvin and Herschey (1993) methodology using the natural logarithm of the ratio of the 52-week high and low stock prices for each firm, an index that is proportional to the Garman and Klass (1980) volatility estimator. We choose this approach over equity beta estimation due to limitation of scope of data availability especially for emerging companies.

σ_k: represents uncertainty underlying the strike price and is determined by the standard deviation of capital expenditures.

α: denotes a second measure of uncertainty in the strike price and represents the cost of hedging that uncertainty $(\alpha_h - \alpha_k)$. It is proxied by the "surprise" or the unanticipated change in the exercise price, and is obtained by ordinary least squares by subtracting the actual percentage change in capital expenditures from the predicted percentage change. In the cross-sectional regression, we don't use this time-series form of the variable. Instead, we derive the "surprise" in capital expenditures as the difference between the natural logarithm of $\left(\dfrac{K_{t+1}}{K_t}\right)$ and that of $\left(\dfrac{K_t}{K_{t-1}}\right)$ where t is current year. Here is the rationale: As of time t, the future change (variance) in capital expenditures is expressed as $\ln\left(\dfrac{K_{t+1}}{K_t}\right)$. And as of time $t-1$, the future change is expressed as $\ln\left(\dfrac{K_t}{K_{t-1}}\right)$. It turns out that any future change in capital expenditures as of time t that was not captured at time $t-1$ is an unexpected change, and represents information at time t that was not available at $t-1$, since *(actual change)* = *(expected change)* + *(unexpected change)*.

D: is debt ratio, the sum of debt in current liabilities and long-term debt divided by total assets, scaled by the industry's debt ratio.

CF: denotes operating cash flow measured by operating income plus R&D expenditures which is meant to proxy internal capital. Another variable used is ΔA, the expected change in assets, a proxy for the net investment component of internal cash flows.

ET: represents the natural logarithm of the number of years the company has lived since it was established. And *L* is a measure of labor productivity, the ratio of total output (net sales) to labor inputs (number of employees).

6.1.4 *Data Sources and Sample Design*

All active U.S. public firms with a record of R&D spending were extracted from the Disclosure CD-ROM. This first sample is restricted to companies within the industries with SIC codes 3000 through 3829. The range covers rubber and miscellaneous plastic products (3000); primary metals (3300); fabricated metals (3400); industrial and commercial machinery and computer equipment (3500); electrical and electronics (3600); transportation equipment (3700); and measuring and controlling devices (3800). Leather and leather products (3100); and stone, clay, glass, concrete products (3200) are excluded.

The companies are then traced as to whether their R&D efforts have turned up any patented innovations. Patent counts come from the Classification and Search Support Information System (CASSIS) CD-ROM, managed by the Patent and Trademark Office of the U.S. Department of Commerce. The database contains bibliographic citations of U.S. patents assigned to individuals, private and public organizations and firms, from 1969 to the present. For our purpose, an entity is considered to have patented if the patent is issued to its subsidiary, division or to the parent firm itself. In most cases CASSIS database would not distinguish a subsidiary from a parent company. For instance, it would list a subsidiary company like Lumec, Inc. and its parent, Thomas Industries, Inc. under completely different assignee codes, often not indicating that Lumec is a subsidiary of Thomas Industries. This is carefully checked.[6]

Information on subsidiaries and divisions of these firms are assembled from several sources for verification purposes: the National Register Publishing's Directory of Corporate Affiliations CD-ROM, Dun and Bradstreet Directory, Walker's Corporate Directory of U.S. Public Companies, and CorpTech Directory of Technology Companies. CASSIS also does not record assignees distinctly as private or public firms. We resolve this problem by cross-checking the CorpTech Directory whose listings identify private and public technology firms as well as foreign-owned companies. Firms that are not cited by CASSIS from 1969 to end of 1993 are not included in the sample. As it turned out, all the companies excluded based on this criterion did not have adequate financial data to analyze and would have again been disqualified.

All data of financial nature are retrieved from the Standard & Poor's annual industrial and full coverage COMPUSTAT tapes. This study covers the period from 1987 to 1993. The final selection of 208 firms constitutes a sample that must have all years of financial data for the period 1987–1993. Year of incorporation (founding) is accessed from Disclosure CD-ROM, Dun and Bradstreet, and CorpTech Directories. The sample is further divided into two panels: established firms and emerging firms. A firm is classified as emerging if it had never issued cash dividends as at end of 1993.

6.1.5 *Industry Classification*

Table 6.1 presents industry classification of the companies to be analyzed. A total of 208 firms make up the final sample of which 107 (51.44%) are emerging and 101 (48.56%) are established firms. Seven major industries are formed according to the two-digit SIC codes. Electrical and Electronics industry accounts for the largest share of the sample with 38.94% of the companies followed by Measuring Instruments and Devices (21.64%) and Industrial and Computer Equipment (21.15%). No emerging company is classified under Rubber and Miscellaneous Plastics (1.44%), and Primary Metals (1.92%), the two industries with the lowest number of firms. The majority of emerging firms (42.99%) are in the Electrical and Electronics industry. Only 1 emerging company compared with 25 mature firms is in the transportation industry, which includes automotive, aircraft and defense. The Measuring Instruments industry is fairly balanced, with 23 emerging and 22 mature firms, respectively.

6.1.6 *Descriptive Statistics*

Figures 6.1 to 6.6 graph some key variables, and descriptive statistics are given in table 5.2. Mature firms are relatively much older, with 1931 being their median year of founding compared with 1975 for emerging companies. Emerging firms on average employ 871 people, ranging from the smallest company with 19 to the largest company with 30,240. On the other hand, mature firms have a mean number of employees of 26,791 ranging from 68 to 354,508.

Table 6.1 Sample Distribution by Industry Classification

2-Digit SIC	Industry	Emerging Firms	Mature Firms	Total	(Percent)
30	Rubber & Miscellaneous Plastics	0	3	3	(1.44)
33	Primary Metals	0	4	4	(1.92)
34	Fabricated Metals and Parts	3	2	5	(2.41)
35	Industrial and Computer Equipment	34	10	44	(21.15)
36	Electrical and Electronics	46	35	81	(38.94)
37	Transportation	1	25	26	(12.50)
38	Measuring Instruments	23	22	45	(21.64)
Total		**107**	**101**	**208**	**(100.00)**

Note: Industry is classified by the two-digit Standard Industrial Classification (SIC) code. Only firms followed by Compustat and cited in CASSIS CD-ROM are included. A company is defined as emerging if it had never issued cash dividends as of December 1993. The sample period is from 1987 to 1993.

Source: Compustat, Disclosure CD-ROM and author's analysis.

Total assets of established firms are about 63 times larger ($4,975 million with a standard deviation of $22,765 million) than those of emerging firms ($78 million with a standard deviation of $208 million). Mature firms also generate almost 52 times as much net sales as emerging firms, $4,217 million against $81 million. However, they have a much lower rate of growth in sales (4.94%) than emerging firms (11.35%). Emerging companies generally spend less in capital expenditures ($8.03 million) and R&D ($9.39 million), compared to mature firms' capital expenditures ($272.14 million) and R&D ($176.71 million). Mature companies experience lower levels of unanticipated changes (surprise) in capital expenditures (−15.94%) than emerging firms (−52.76%).

Figure 6.1 Number of Patents Granted to Emerging and Mature Firms, 1969–1995

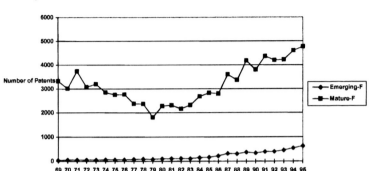

Source: CASSIS CD-ROM (PTO) and author's analysis.

On average, there are 3 patents procured by an emerging firm per year compared to 39 by a mature company. For each patent assigned, a mature firm spends $4.5 million in R&D. This is higher than $2.9 million incurred by an emerging firm.

Debt ratios don't appear to be significantly different between the two subsamples, 21.51% and 18.87% for mature and emerging firms, respectively. In terms of investment volatility, emerging companies are much riskier, with the natural logarithm of the ratio

Figure 6.2 Mean Net Sales at 1987 Dollars (in Millions)

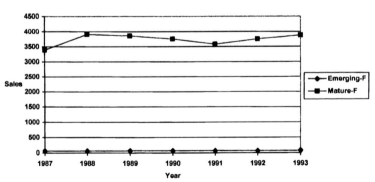

Source: Compustat and author's analysis.

Figure 6.3 Net Sales Per Employee at 1987 Dollars (in Millions)

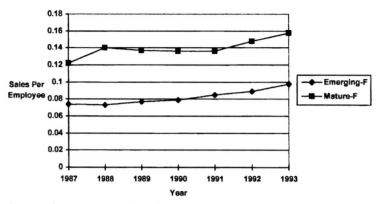

Source: Compustat and author's analysis.

of the 52-week high to 52-week low of stock price of 0.422 compared to 0.267 for mature firms. Established companies enjoy higher levels of operating cash flows ($492 million) compared to that of emerging firms ($13 million). On average, emerging companies register a much higher ratio of excess value (growth opportunities) to book value of assets (63%) than established companies (7%). Mature firms tend to operate in more highly concentrated industries with Herfindhal-Hirschman index of about 2200 while

Figure 6.4 R&D Expenditure at 1987 Dollars (in Millions)

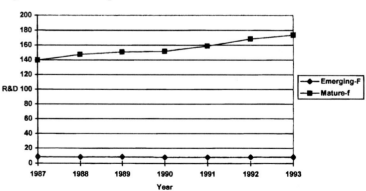

Source: Compustat and author's analysis.

Figure 6.5 Mean Capital Expenditure at 1987 Dollars (in Million)

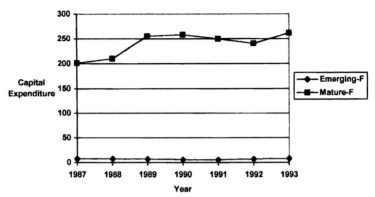

Source: Compustat and author's analysis.

emerging companies are in more diffused industries at about 1500 level of the same index.

6.2 Empirical Results

In Table 6.3 we present tests of significance of the mean difference of selected variables in the two subsamples. Both t-Tests and

Figure 6.6 R&D Per Patent Granted at 1987 Dollars (in Millions)

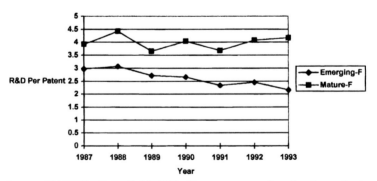

Source: CASSIS CD-ROM (PTO), Compustat and author's analysis.

Table 6.2 Descriptive Statistics for Selected Variables

Time-series means of variables computed over the period 1987 to 1993 (standard deviation in parenthesis). Year of incorporation is median year. Patents are in units. Employees are in thousands. Volatility of the growth option is computed as the natural logarithm of the ratio of the 52-week high to 52-week low of the stock price as in Chauvin & Hirschey (1993) following Garman & Klass (1980). Growth rates of sales and R&D are derived by simple exponential trend regression and are percentages. "Surprise" is the unanticipated change in capital expenditures obtained by ordinary least squares by subtracting the actual from predicted percentage change. Rival R&D is obtained by subtracting firm R&D from industry R&D. Operating cash flow is measured by operating income plus R&D expenditures. Debt ratio is the sum of debt in current liabilities and long-term debt divided by total assets. Herfindhal-Hirschman index, a measure of industry concentration, is calculated by summing the squares of percent market share of each firm (using sales) in the industry. Growth opportunities is the excess market value over replacement cost of the firm, computed as the sum of the market value of equity and total debt less total book assets. Net sales, total assets, capital expenditures, R&D, rival R&D, operating cash flow and growth opportunities are in millions of dollars. Industry is classified by the two-digit SIC code.

Variable	Emerging Firms	Mature Firms	All Firms
Year Founded	1975	1931	1964
Employees	0.871	6.791	13.458
	(3.219)	(87.533)	(62.252)
Net sales	80.884	4216.591	2089.088
	(232.298)	(15811.640)	(11184.700)
Growth Rate of Sales	11.354	4.943	8.241
	(23.378)	(9.323)	(18.226)
Total Assets	78.160	4975.058	2455.981
	(208.248)	(22764.980)	(16012.520)
Capital Expenditures	8.028	272.141	136.275
	(29.737)	(1128.795)	(795.932)
Surprise in Capita Exp.	−52.762	−15.938	−34.881
	(80.366)	(28.160)	(63.488)
R&D Expenditures	9.393	176.714	90.640
	(32.441)	(665.688)	(470.790)

Table 6.2 (*Continued*)

Variable	Emerging Firms	Mature Firms	All Firms
Growth Rate of R&D	7.762	6.856	7.322
	(16.399)	(13.182)	(14.895)
Rival R&D	1987.139	4648.871	3279.615
	(1806.186)	(4880.103)	(3867.023)
Patents	3.215	39.122	20.153
	(10.832)	(91.468)	(66.524)
Stock of Patents	21.965	467.440	238.278
	(68.358)	(1035.636)	(755.208)
Debt Ratio	18.874	21.507	20.153
	(19.056)	(14.312)	(16.931)
Operating Cash Flow	12.780	491.506	245.239
	(42.632)	(1879.365)	(1328.436)
Project Volatility	0.422	0.267	0.347
	(0.116)		(0.130)
Herfindhal-Hirschman Index	1521	2205	1853
Growth Opportunities	3.809	-817.555	-395.026
	(52.908)	(10000.600)	(6963.168)

Wilcoxon non-parametric approximations are performed. The results are very similar employing both methods. We find 8 of the 14 variables (without their change components) considered are significantly different between the emerging and mature firm groups. In particular, the difference in growth opportunities (G_t) is highly significant, strongly supporting the hypothesis that emerging firms have distinctively larger real options than mature firms. On average, 63% of the market value of emerging firms compared to 7% for mature firms is accounted for by the present value of growth opportunities. Mean differences of stock of patents (PP), R&D (X), rival R&D (Y), project risk (σ_v), capital expenditures (K), operating cash flows (CF), and industry concentration (HH) are all significant. We infer that emerging firms are in high R&D industries, less concentrated, more volatile with less free-cash-flow and higher Tobin's Q ratio.

Table 6.3 *t*-Tests and Non-Parametric Comparisons of Mean Differences

The non-parametric procedure is the Wilcoxon Normal Approximation. Industry is defined by the 2-digit SIC code. ΔA and CF are meant to proxy for internal capital. CF denotes operating cash flow measured by operating income plus R&D expenditures. ΔA is the annual change in total assets, a proxy for the net investment component of internal capital. ΔS is annual change (expected growth) in net sales. HH represents the Herfindhal-Hirschman index, calculated by summing the squares of percent market share of each firm (using sales) in the industry. Both ΔS and HH are meant to proxy for the expected value of the monopoly rents. P denotes the relative probability of innovation derived as the number of patents divided by the industry number of patents, and PP is stock of patents, computed by dividing cumulative patents within past 17 years by industry stock of patents, both scaled by the ratio of firm assets to industry assets. σ_v represents volatility of the growth option, computed as the natural logarithm of the ratio of the 52-week high to 52-week low of the stock price as in Chauvin & Hirschey (1993) following Garman & Klass (1980). K denotes capital expenditure, and α_k is the "surprise" or unexpected change in capital expenditures derived as the difference between $Log(K_{t+1}/K_t)$ and $Log(K_t/K_{t-1})$ where t is current year. X represents R&D. Y denotes rival R&D obtained by subtracting firm R&D from industry R&D, normalized by industry assets. Labor productivity, L, is the ratio of total output (net sales) to labor inputs (number of employees). Debt ratio, D, is the sum of debt in current liabilities and long-term debt divided by total assets, scaled by industry debt ratio. G denotes the excess market value over replacement cost of the firm, a proxy for growth opportunities, and is computed as the sum of the market value of equity and total debt less total book assets. ΔA, CF, ΔS, X, K, and G are all normalized by assets.

Variable	Emerging Firms	Mature Firms	t-Statistic	Z-Statistic
ΔA	0.0990	0.0735	−0.5452	0.4076
ΔS	0.1442	0.0814	−1.2472	−0.4889
P	2.5000	1.5403	−1.3429	1.1848
PP	1.8119	1.8588	0.2132	2.1655**
X	0.1302	0.0543	−5.7884***	−7.0179***
Y	0.0707	0.0577	−5.1853***	−4.8589***

Table 6.3 (*Continued*)

Variable	Emerging Firms	Mature Firms	t-Statistic	Z-Statistic
K	0.0602	0.0607	0.0929	1.8790**
α_k	−0.0461	−0.0034	0.3527	0.6159
L	11.8264	11.0063	−0.9725	−1.1410
D	0.9682	0.9029	−0.4804	0.7226
CF	0.0791	0.1437	2.3884**	1.3895
HH	1552	2216	3.5576***	3.8258***
σ_v	1.0017	0.6375	−6.5193***	−6.8092***
G	0.6262	0.0566	−2.9683***	−2.4006**

*** Significance at the 0.01 level in a two-tailed test.
** Significance at the 0.05 level in a two-tailed test.
* Significance at the 0.10 level in a two-tailed test.

Cross-sectional regressions are then conducted. We regress excess market value on relevant predictor variables as indicated and present results for the one-year change regressions in Tables 6.4 and 6.5. We also run regressions with current patents as dependent variable and present results in Tables 6.6 and 6.7. It is apparent that the impact and signs of some predictor variables in explaining the changes in the dependent variable do change from period to period. However, an overall picture of the power of a particular factor can be discerned.

There is evidence that current (X_t), past (ΔX_{t-1}) and future (ΔX_{t+1}) expected values of R&D for emerging firms are positively significant. On the contrary, current and future expected R&D expenditures for mature firms are negative and significant for the most part. Although they lose their power in some periods, patents (P_t) have value.

Current (Y_t) and past (ΔY_{t-1}) rival R&D tend to be positive, but future rival R&D (ΔY_{t+1}) are negative for emerging firms. For mature firms, rival R&D are generally positive.

One salient result is the influence of internal cash flows. For emerging companies, the net investment components of internal capital (ΔA_{t-1} and ΔA_{t+1}) are positive and significant. Current (CF_t)

Table 6.4 One-year Change Cross-sectional Regression Analysis with Excess Value, G_t, as Dependent Variable

Mean coefficients and their t-statistics from simple regressions run for each year t across all firms. INT denotes intercept and ET is the natural logarithm of the number of years of life of a firm since founded. All other variables are as defined in table 6.3. A firm must have data on all variables in the seven-year sample period, 1987–1993. Future change (one-year) in R&D is expressed as: $\Delta X_{t+1} = (X_{t+1} - X_t)/A_t$. Past change (one-year) in R&D is expressed as: $\Delta X_{t-1} = (X_t - X_{t-1})/A_t$. Changes (expected values) in all other variables are computed similarly and scaled as defined in table 6.3, except for L, α, and HH which are ratio changes.

Panel A: Emerging Firms

Variable	1988		1989		1990		1991		1992		Fama-MacBeth Regression	
	Coeff.	t-stat.	Coeff.	t-stat.	Coeff.	t-stat.	Coeff.	t-stat.	Coeff.	t-stat.	Coeff.	t-stat.
INT	-7.273	-0.254	105.722	3.893***	0.241	0.012	-8.087	-0.437	-9.701	-0.905	16.180	1.081
ET	-0.424	-2.612***	-0.753	-3.098***	-0.355	-1.318	-0.260	-1.069	-0.334	-1.303	-0.425	-3.409***
ΔA_{t+1}	1.060	1.677*	1.000	1.127	0.594	1.371	1.608	1.714*	0.779	1.350	1.008	2.759***
ΔA_{t-1}	3.656	5.413***	3.417	3.479***	-0.192	-0.208	3.207	3.843***	1.348	1.545	2.287	5.925***
ΔS_{t+1}	0.864	1.457	-0.594	-0.640	0.456	0.753	-1.116	-1.536	0.384	0.673	-0.001	0.283
ΔS_{t-1}	-1.004	-1.732**	-0.101	-0.114	0.349	0.469	0.685	1.314	-0.509	-0.641	-0.116	-0.072
P_t	-0.018	-0.562	-0.038	-0.926	-0.005	-0.262	0.038	0.859	-0.015	-0.373	-0.008	-0.505
PP_t	-0.016	-0.256	0.073	1.092	-0.010	-0.143	-0.006	-0.121	-0.004	-0.112	0.007	0.184
ΔP_{t+1}	0.025	0.820	-0.028	-0.856	0.004	0.086	-0.013	-0.308	-0.031	-0.725	-0.009	-0.394
X_t	3.148	1.810**	1.765	0.845	1.814	1.185	4.954	3.003***	7.044	3.683***	3.745	4.210***
ΔX_{t+1}	-5.138	-2.710***	19.041	5.357***	1.656	0.376	9.783	2.305**	6.365	1.190	6.342	2.895***
ΔX_{t-1}	5.674	1.464	5.087	1.309	7.890	2.271**	-2.789	-1.074	8.346	2.042**	4.842	2.404**

Table 6.4 (Continued)

Panel A: Emerging Firms

Variable	1988 Coeff.	1988 t-stat.	1989 Coeff.	1989 t-stat.	1990 Coeff.	1990 t-stat.	1991 Coeff.	1991 t-stat.	1992 Coeff.	1992 t-stat.	Fama-MacBeth Regression Coeff.	Fama-MacBeth Regression t-stat.
Y_t	37.179	0.375	-407.6	-3.727***	25.451	0.178	26.565	0.255	142.63	1.094	-35.154	-0.730
ΔY_{t+1}	-446.43	-0.966	912.3	3.255***	-283.7	-0.528	322.95	0.650	-859.9	-1.548	-70.96	0.345
ΔY_{t-1}	607.99	0.935	-1190	-2.636***	228.2	0.643	-190.61	-0.346	-341.9	-0.507	-177.3	-0.765
K_t	-0.113	-0.045	-2.857	-0.884	0.365	0.113	-2.251	-0.774	0.570	0.193	-0.679	-0.559
ΔK_{t+1}	1.478	0.719	-0.439	-0.132	-1.429	-0.343	-1.872	-0.524	-7.895	-1.647	-2.031	-0.771
ΔK_{t-1}	-0.770	-0.246	8.893	2.075**	3.658	1.071	-3.764	-0.999	4.375	1.193	2.478	1.238
α_t	-0.104	-1.752*	0.525	3.151***	0.081	0.527	-0.087	-0.699	0.189	1.492	0.121	1.087
L_t	0.009	1.792*	-0.005	-0.726	0.002	0.390	-0.004	-0.854	0.000	0.027	0.000	0.252
ΔL_{t+1}	-0.007	-1.613	0.008	1.300	-0.001	-0.323	-0.002	-0.314	0.003	0.732	0.000	-0.227
ΔL_{t-1}	-0.003	-0.891	-0.004	-0.485	-0.002	-0.285	0.009	2.494**	0.001	0.236	0.000	0.427
D_t	0.057	0.395	-0.127	-0.718	-0.293	-1.434	-0.043	-0.290	-0.044	-0.350	-0.090	-0.958
ΔD_{t+1}	-0.644	-4.067***	-0.333	-1.004	-0.796	-1.661*	0.241	0.923	0.153	1.050	-0.276	-1.903*
ΔD_{t-1}	-0.505	-2.728***	-0.037	-0.166	0.446	1.365	-0.630	-1.731*	-0.219	-0.673	-0.189	-1.573
CF_t	-3.550	-4.728***	-5.618	-6.042***	-3.312	-3.308***	-2.702	-2.299**	-6.378	-5.095***	-4.312	-8.589***
ΔCF_{t+1}	-1.114	-1.517	-0.398	-0.274	-2.322	-2.096**	1.390	0.750	-2.838	-2.496**	-1.057	-2.253*
ΔCF_{t-1}	0.876	0.855	-2.201	-2.179**	2.255	2.292**	-0.728	-1.044	3.651	2.420**	0.771	0.937
HH_t	0.003	0.229	-0.049	-3.644***	-0.001	-0.059	0.004	0.513	0.002	0.756	-0.008	-0.882

Table 6.4 (Continued)

| | Panel A: Emerging Firms | | | | | | | | | | Fama-MacBeth Regression | |
| | 1988 | | 1989 | | 1990 | | 1991 | | 1992 | | | |
Variable	Coeff.	t-stat.	Coeff.	t-stat.	Coeff.	t-stat.	Coeff.	t-stat.	Coeff.	t-stat.	Coeff.	t-stat.
ΔHH_{t+1}	0.005	0.131	−0.290	−2.999***	0.010	0.231	−0.008	−0.611	0.093	1.557	−0.038	−0.677
ΔHH_{t-1}	0.007	1.057	−0.037	−1.902*	−0.020	−0.291	0.012	0.538	−0.031	−1.424	−0.014	−0.809
σ_t	0.035	0.083	0.272	0.588	−0.252	−0.489	0.327	0.836	−0.087	−0.209	0.059	0.324
$\Delta\sigma_{t+1}$	−0.050	−0.184	−0.768	−2.179**	0.129	0.315	0.469	1.488	−0.109	−0.349	−0.066	−0.364
$\Delta\sigma_{t-1}$	0.440	0.297	−0.413	−1.250	−0.368	−0.986	0.568	1.681*	0.192	0.084	0.084	0.134
Adj. R^2	0.674		0.815		0.475		0.507		0.613			
F-Stat.	7.63***		15.2**		3.90***		4.30***		6.1***		7.42***	

*** Significance at the 0.01 level in a two-tailed test.

** Significance at the 0.05 level in a two-tailed test.

* Significance at the 0.10 level in a two-tailed test.

Table 6.5 One-year Change Cross-Sectional Regression Analysis with Excess Value, G_v as Dependent Variable

Mean coefficients and their t-statistics from simple regressions run for each year t across all firms. INT denotes intercept and ET is the natural logarithm of the number of years of life of a firm since founded. All other variables are as defined in table 6.3. A firm must have data on all variables in the seven-year sample period, 1987–1993. Future change (one-year) in R&D is expressed as: $\Delta X_{t+1} = (X_{t+1} - X_t)/A_t$. Past change (one-year) in R&D is expressed as: $\Delta X_{t-1} = (X_t - X_{t-1})/A_t$. Changes (expected values) in all other variables are computed similarly and scaled as defined in table 6.3, except for L, α, and HH which are ratio changes.

Panel B: Mature Firms

Variable	1988 Coeff.	1988 t-stat.	1989 Coeff.	1989 t.stat.	1990 Coeff.	1990 t-stat.	1991 Coeff.	1991 t-stat.	1992 Coeff.	1992 t-stat.	Fama-MacBeth Regression Coeff.	Fama-MacBeth Regression t-stat.
INT	-0.177	-0.292	-1.018	-1.675*	-0.824	-0.879	0.873	0.703	0.411	0.419	-0.091	-0.617
ET	-0.177	-1.827*	-0.164	-1.780*	-0.211	-2.036**	-0.449	-2.303**	-0.462	-2.766***	-0.293	-4.285***
ΔA_{t-1}	-0.804	-2.350**	-0.385	-0.821	-1.236	-1.978**	1.918	1.541	-1.213	-1.689*	-0.344	-1.794*
ΔA_{t-1}	-0.419	-1.119	0.322	0.744	-0.229	-0.509	-1.147	-1.124	0.323	0.303	-0.230	-0.682
ΔS_{t+1}	0.348	1.079	-0.274	-0.599	0.076	0.255	-0.893	-1.120	2.249	3.074***	0.301	1.331
ΔS_{t-1}	0.373	0.850	0.432	1.270	-0.303	-0.665	-0.080	-0.132	-0.480	-0.783	-0.098	0.216
P_t	-0.031	-1.091	-0.010	-0.389	0.012	0.413	-0.039	-0.631	-0.056	-0.861	-0.025	-1.024
PP_t	-0.023	-0.863	0.001	0.022	-0.030	-1.272	-0.069	-2.079**	-0.040	-1.052	-0.032	-1.122
ΔP_{t+1}	0.023	1.289	0.019	0.540	0.023	0.685	0.151	2.636***	0.123	2.525**	0.068	2.015**
X_t	-2.908	-2.049**	-5.232	-3.353***	-6.815	-4.515***	-9.495	-3.815***	-9.090	-3.935***	-6.708	-7.066***
ΔX_{t+1}	-9.207	-2.570**	0.413	0.119	-4.767	-1.064	4.649	0.834	-26.65	-4.609***	-7.112	-2.891***
ΔX_{t-1}	4.036	1.223	-3.931	-1.121	4.563	1.601	-3.154	-0.430	13.09	2.564**	2.922	1.535

Table 6.5 (Continued)

Panel B: Mature Firms

Variable	1988 Coeff.	t-stat.	1989 Coeff.	t.stat.	1990 Coeff.	t-stat.	1991 Coeff.	t-stat.	1992 Coeff.	t-stat.	Fama-MacBeth Regression Coeff.	t-stat.
Y_t	-0.840	-0.229	2.880	0.764	3.966	0.677	-15.637	-1.183	5.181	0.459	-0.890	0.098
ΔY_{t+1}	-12.533	-0.269	28.990	1.898*	-15.480	-0.190	28.908	0.470	32.22	0.658	12.421	1.027
ΔY_{t-1}	41.725	0.985	1.678	0.044	44.741	0.959	184.29	1.669*	-13.47	-0.143	51.792	1.405
K_t	2.224	1.401	0.889	0.582	4.571	2.836***	4.126	1.449	5.568	1.981**	3.475	3.300***
ΔK_{t+1}	0.794	0.390	0.984	0.357	8.290	3.270***	2.491	0.499	-2.487	-0.604	2.014	1.565
ΔK_{t-1}	-1.318	-0.501	1.312	0.518	-2.654	-0.884	5.894	1.221	-1.016	-0.267	0.444	0.035
α_t	-0.043	-0.376	0.122	1.123	-0.211	-1.717*	0.224	0.980	0.041	0.240	0.026	0.100
L_t	-0.001	-0.076	-0.001	-0.089	0.011	2.424**	0.004	0.388	0.003	0.465	0.003	1.245
ΔL_{t+1}	0.001	0.207	0.005	1.334	-0.004	-1.093	-0.009	-1.413	-0.004	-0.742	-0.001	-0.683
ΔL_{t-1}	0.002	0.496	-0.004	-0.777	-0.007	-2.148**	0.009	1.270	0.005	0.716	0.001	-0.110
D_t	0.202	2.239**	0.149	1.728*	0.029	0.340	-0.101	-1.197	-0.196	-1.667*	0.016	0.577
ΔD_{t+1}	0.137	1.274	0.061	0.672	-0.207	-1.513	-0.235	-0.666	-0.192	-0.790	-0.163	-0.409
ΔD_{t-1}	-0.169	-1.114	-0.128	-0.898	0.200	1.453	0.224	0.913	0.043	0.132	0.034	0.195
CF_t	4.281	4.542***	7.078	7.471***	6.663	6.939***	6.943	4.155***	6.082	4.073***	6.210	10.872***
ΔCF_{t+1}	0.808	0.817	0.727	0.781	3.412	3.393***	1.728	0.741	2.878	1.538	1.910	4.398***
ΔCF_{t-1}	0.332	0.298	-3.660	-2.901***	-3.339	-2.737***	1.728	0.741	2.848	1.563*	-0.418	-1.214

Table 6.5 (Continued)

Panel B: Mature Firms

Variable	1988 Coeff.	t-stat.	1989 Coeff.	t.stat.	1990 Coeff.	t-stat.	1991 Coeff.	t-stat.	1992 Coeff.	t-stat.	Fama-MacBeth Regression Coeff.	t-stat.
HH_t	-0.000	-0.204	0.0001	1.690*	0.000	0.785	0.000	0.402	0.000	0.579	0.000	1.095
ΔHH_{t+1}	-0.001	-0.768	-0.001	-0.614	0.003	1.063	-0.006	-1.527	-0.001	-0.318	-0.001	-0.866
ΔHH_{t-1}	0.001	1.324	0.001	0.960	-0.004	-0.998	0.000	0.069	-0.003	-0.971	-0.001	-0.154
σ_t	-0.406	-1.558	0.114	0.519	-0.011	-0.062	0.767	2.279**	0.397	1.356	0.172	1.013
$\Delta \sigma_{t+1}$	-0.104	-0.675	0.074	0.402	-0.046	-0.301	0.782	2.460**	-0.181	-0.853	0.105	0.413
$\Delta \sigma_{t-1}$	0.167	0.721	-0.083	-0.401	0.148	0.960	0.444	1.523	-0.187	-0.627	0.098	0.733
Adj. R^2	0.424		0.573		0.573		0.580		0.605			
F-Stat.	3.2***		5.1***		5.1***		5.2***		5.7***		4.86***	

*** Significance at the 0.01 level in a two-tailed test.
** Significance at the 0.05 level in a two-tailed test.
* Significance at the 0.10 level in a two-tailed test.

Table 6.6 One-year Change Cross-Sectional Regression Analysis with Current Patents, P_t as Dependent Variable

Mean coefficients and their t-statistics from simple regressions run for each year t across all firms. INT denotes intercept and ET is the natural logarithm of the number of years of life of a firm since founded. All other variables are as defined in table 6.3. A firm must have data on all variables in the seven-year sample period, 1987–1993. Future change (one-year) in R&D is expressed as: $\Delta X_{t+1} = (X_{t+1} - X_t)/A_t$. Past change (one-year) in R&D is expressed as: $\Delta X_{t-1} = (X_t - X_{t-1})/A_t$. Changes (expected values) in all other variables are computed similarly and scaled as defined in table 6.3, except for L, α, and HH which are ratio changes.

Panel A: Emerging Firms

Variable	1988 Coeff.	1988 t-stat.	1989 Coeff.	1989 t.stat.	1990 Coeff.	1990 t-stat.	1991 Coeff.	1991 t-stat.	1992 Coeff.	1992 t-stat.	Fama-Macbeth Regression Coeff.	Fama-Macbeth Regression t-stat.
INT	-102.5	-0.995	-46.811	-1.435	5.021	0.056	89.955	2.032**	7.289	0.353	-9.417	0.004
ET	-1.078	-1.882**	-0.766	-1.154	-1.870	-1.207	-0.871	-1.381	-1.684	-2.405**	-1.254	-3.212***
ΔA_{t+1}	0.238	0.119	5.064	3.086***	0.152	0.059	-3.705	-2.003**	-1.014	-0.728	0.147	0.213
ΔA_{t-1}	3.099	1.427	3.189	1.274	-11.99	-2.694***	1.336	0.671	1.283	0.521	-0.617	0.480
ΔS_{t+1}	-2.329	-1.406	1.753	1.071	-0.288	-0.127	2.562	2.129**	1.305	1.036	0.601	1.081
ΔS_{t-1}	0.792	0.392	-3.943	-1.812	10.292	2.627	0.723	0.529	-0.196	-0.094	1.534	0.657
PP_t	0.315	1.496	0.354	2.066**	0.993	2.385**	0.825	9.240***	0.281	3.203***	0.554	7.356***
ΔP_{t+1}	0.384	4.128***	-0.043	-0.472	-0.266	-0.946	0.199	2.184**	0.196	1.802*	0.094	2.678***
X_t	7.006	1.119	14.556	2.828***	16.661	1.826*	4.160	1.311	1.093	0.246	8.695	2.932***
ΔX_{t-1}	-13.45	-1.155	-16.713	-1.598	28.469	1.371	-0.776	-0.116	32.758	3.203***	6.057	0.681
Y_t	327.3	0.930	361.7	1.891*	65.097	0.101	-735.7	-2.922***	-183.9	-0.725	-33.10	-0.290
ΔY_{t-1}	1277	0.832	1485	1.216	483.3	0.239	876.9	0.848	2765	1.561	1377	1.878*
K_t	21.702	2.640***	-6.903	-0.855	-8.144	-0.438	2.675	0.357	-10.34	-1.296	-0.202	0.163

Table 6.6 (Continued)

| | Panel A: Emerging Firms | | | | | | | | | | | Fama-Macbeth Regression | |
| | 1988 | | 1989 | | 1990 | | 1991 | | 1992 | | | |
Variable	Coeff.	t-stat.	Coeff.	t-stat.	Coeff.	t-stat.	Coeff.	t-stat.	Coeff.	t-stat.	Coeff.	t-stat.
ΔK_{t-1}	-10.432	-1.008	-8.170	-0.724	23.389	1.171*	-1.569	-0.163	1.328	0.128	0.909	-0.238
α_t	0.536	3.224***	-0.556	-1.375	-0.041	-0.056	0.342	1.180	-0.091	-0.296	0.040	1.071
L_t	0.001	0.107	-0.018	-1.056	-0.009	-0.323	-0.007	-1.101	-0.004	-0.257	-0.007	-1.052
ΔL_{t-1}	0.000	0.017	0.013	0.741	0.002	0.058	0.020	2.398**	0.001	0.067	0.007	1.312
D_t	-0.414	-0.826	-0.302	-0.684	-0.316	-0.288	-0.046	-0.124	0.111	0.310	-0.193	-0.645
ΔD_{t-1}	-0.633	-1.002	0.895	1.520	-3.042	-1.620	0.034	0.037	-0.419	-0.519	-0.633	-0.634
CF_t	-4.131	-1.637	0.533	0.224	0.958	0.172	-4.452	-2.052**	-0.937	-0.277	-1.606	-1.428
ΔCF_{t-1}	-2.477	-0.721	2.424	0.913	-4.268	-0.787	6.206	3.675***	4.996	1.257	1.376	1.735*
HH_t	0.046	1.063	0.012	1.118	-0.005	-0.167	-0.025	-1.534	0.002	0.408	0.006	0.355
ΔHH_{t+1}	0.152	1.218	-0.047	-1.285	-0.016	-0.095	-0.018	-0.948	-0.072	-1.729*	-0.008	-1.136
ΔHH_{t-1}	0.001	0.119	-0.047	-1.472	-0.106	-0.323	-0.034	-0.681	-0.028	-1.189	-0.043	-1.430
σ_t	0.159	0.134	-0.647	-0.574	-0.037	-0.015	-1.524	-1.844*	-1.046	-0.986	-0.619	-1.314
$\Delta \sigma_{t-1}$	0.298	0.297	0.351	0.397	-1.268	-0.566	2.350	2.931***	2.090	2.345**	0.764	2.162**
$Adj. R^2$	0.542		0.486		0.311		0.781		0.382			
F-Stat.	6.0***		5.0***		2.9**		16.1***		3.6***		6.7***	

*** Significance at the 0.01 level in a two-tailed test.
** Significance at the 0.05 level in a two-tailed test.
* Significance at the 0.10 level in a two-tailed test.

Table 6.7 One-year Change Cross-Sectional Regression Analysis with Current Patents, P_t as Dependent Variable

Mean coefficients and their t-statistics from simple regressions run for each year t across all firms. INT denotes intercept and ET is the natural logarithm of the number of years of life of a firm since founded. All other variables are as defined in table 6.3. A firm must have data on all variables in the seven-year sample period, 1987–1993. Future change (one-year) in R&D is expressed as: $\Delta X_{t+1} = (X_{t+1} - X_t)/A_t$. Past change (one-year) in R&D is expressed as: $\Delta X_{t-1} = (X_t - X_{t-1})/A_t$. Changes (expected values) in all other variables are computed similarly and scaled as defined in table 6.3, except for L, α, and HH which are ratio changes.

Panel B: Mature Firms

Variable	1988 Coeff.	1988 t-stat.	1989 Coeff.	1989 t.stat.	1990 Coeff.	1990 t-stat.	1991 Coeff.	1991 t-stat.	1992 Coeff.	1992 t-stat.	Fama-Macbeth Regression Coeff.	Fama-Macbeth Regression t-stat.
INT	3.995	1.709*	-4.745	-1.768*	-2.874	-0.944	4.140	1.985**	-0.278	-0.150	0.048	0.333
ET	-0.174	-0.484	0.246	0.594	0.403	1.123	0.135	0.376	0.043	0.137	0.131	0.698
ΔA_{t+1}	-0.130	-0.113	-0.019	-0.017	1.432	0.786	0.868	0.630	1.056	0.932	0.641	0.887
ΔA_{t-1}	-1.728	-1.166	-1.669	-0.952	0.855	0.480	-1.120	-0.596	0.616	0.321	-0.609	-0.765
ΔS_{t+1}	-1.619	-1.679*	-1.293	-0.757	0.340	0.355	-0.796	-0.737	0.103	0.107	-0.653	-1.084
ΔS_{t-1}	1.849	1.078	3.015	2.063**	-1.820	-1.058	1.111	1.066	0.545	0.514	0.940	1.465
PP_t	-0.087	-0.837	0.211	1.711*	0.513	7.207***	0.115	1.969*	0.137	2.027**	0.178	4.831***
ΔP_{t+1}	0.285	4.398***	0.905	8.543***	0.586	5.222***	0.375	4.304***	0.557	8.408**	0.542	12.35***
X_t	0.126	0.023	28.126	4.536**	6.401	1.319	-3.113	-0.750	2.124	0.514	6.733	2.257**
ΔX_{t-1}	6.656	0.569	-51.47	-3.970**	4.796	0.439	14.141	1.189	-26.67	-3.249***	-10.51	-2.009**
Y_t	-40.324	-2.944***	14.998	0.891	28.062	1.402	-52.22	-2.885***	-6.376	-0.298	-11.17	-1.534
ΔY_{t-1}	22.271	0.234	138.9	0.937	-117.2	-0.963	267.7	1.418	92.569	0.608	80.86	0.894
K_t	10.707	1.730*	-5.705	-0.840	-6.292	-1.099	5.555	1.052	0.410	0.080	0.935	0.369

Table 6.7 (Continued)

Panel B: Mature Firms

Variable	1988 Coeff.	1988 t-stat.	1989 Coeff.	1989 t.stat.	1990 Coeff.	1990 t-stat.	1991 Coeff.	1991 t-stat.	1992 Coeff.	1992 t-stat.	Fama-Macbeth Regression Coeff.	Fama-Macbeth Regression t-stat.
ΔK_{t-1}	−14.739	−1.595	−5.941	−0.523	3.240	0.301	−5.017	−0.694	10.43	1.508	−2.405	−0.401
α_t	−0.157	−0.452	0.024	0.067	−0.257	−0.707	−0.197	−0.721	0.221	0.952	−0.073	−0.344
L_t	−0.012	−0.871	−0.035	−1.823	0.021	1.673*	−0.012	−1.004	0.011	1.194	−0.006	−0.332
ΔL_{t-1}	0.010	0.640	0.042	2.003**	−0.017	−1.424	0.006	0.469	−0.016	−1.454	0.005	0.094
D_t	−0.231	−0.644	−0.472	−1.330	0.272	0.924	−0.144	−0.942	0.492	2.446**	−0.017	0.935
ΔD_{t-1}	0.006	0.011	−0.494	−0.848	−0.229	−0.417	0.147	0.360	−0.621	−1.008	−0.238	−0.761
CF_t	0.493	0.145	−1.959	−0.474	−4.644	−1.341	−0.882	−0.310	5.717	2.254**	−0.255	0.110
ΔCF_{t-1}	−0.225	−0.051	9.198	1.656*	4.140	0.874	0.314	0.115	−9.582	−3.157***	0.769	−0.225
HH_t	−0.000	−2.401**	0.001	1.651	0.000	0.702	−0.000	−2.887***	0.000	0.899	0.000	−0.814
ΔHH_{t+1}	−0.001	−0.130	−0.006	−0.702	−0.002	−0.232	−0.005	−0.804	−0.004	−1.033	−0.003	−1.160
ΔHH_{t-1}	0.002	1.298	0.006	0.725	0.007	0.444	0.003	0.621	0.004	0.834	0.004	1.569
σ_t	0.352	0.359	1.153	1.270	−1.057	−1.529	−0.068	−0.137	−0.710	−1.376	−0.066	−0.565
$\Delta \sigma_{t-1}$	−0.614	−0.713	−0.250	−0.283	0.615	1.154	0.204	0.374	1.022	2.027**	0.195	1.024
Adj. R^2	0.432		0.821		0.759		0.591		0.795			
F-Stat.	4.1***		19.4***		13.6***		6.8***		16.5**		12.1***	

*** Significance at the 0.01 level in a two-tailed test.
** Significance at the 0.05 level in a two-tailed test.
* Significance at the 0.10 level in a two-tailed test.

and future values (ΔCF_{t+1}) of operating cash flows are significantly negative, and past values (ΔCF_{t-1}) are positive. These results strongly support our internal capital markets hypothesis. High Tobin's Q firms are high investment firms. And since for emerging companies investments must be financed internally, it implies that high Q emerging firms would have less cash flow left over after investments.

The negative sign of current operating cash flows for emerging firms also tends to support Jensen's (1986) assertion that after all positive NPV projects are considered and financed, and shareholders paid, the remaining "free cash flows" are often "wasted" by management. On the other hand, operating cash flows for mature firms are positive and highly significant, but the net investment component is negative for most of the sample period. There could be additional explanations for our results.[7]

For emerging firms, capital expenditure (K) signs are mixed, but generally show a negative relationship with growth opportunities in the two-year regressions. Unexpected values have positive signs in two of three regressions. Mature firms show a positive relationship of capital expenditures and their unexpected values with growth opportunities, overall.

Volatility of the underlying investments (σ_v) has positive relationship in both sub-samples for most of the study period. Debt ratio (D) has a negative sign for emerging firms, but the signs are mixed for the established firms.

Tables 6.6 and 6.7 show that the change in innovation, measured by the current number of patents (P_t) is significantly explained by the stock of patents (PP_t), R&D (X_t), and research-in-progress as proxied by expected future changes in the number of patents (ΔP_{t+1}). Operating cash flows (CF_t) and rival R&D (Y_t) have greater impact on innovation in emerging than in mature firms.

6.3 The Fama-French Methodology

We next apply a cross-sectional regression approach proposed by Fama and French (1997), following Fama and MacBeth (1973), in determining influencing variables on the valuation of growth opportunities of a firm to verify our findings. The Fama-MacBeth regressions have the following form:

$$G_{i,t} = \mu_0 + \sum_{j=1}^{H} \mu_{j,t} F_{i,j,t} + e_{i,t} \text{ for } i = 1, 2, \dots, N_t \quad (28)$$

where H is the number of explanatory variables, N is the number of firms, and $F_{i,j,t}$ is the realization of explanatory factor j for firm i in year t ($t = 1, 2, \dots, T$). Our sample period remains 1987–1993. We test the null hypothesis that the time-series average of year-by-year regression slopes is zero. That is,

$$\frac{\sum_{t=1} \mu_{j,t}}{T} = 0 \text{ for } j = 1, 2, \dots, T. \quad (29)$$

A t-test that assumes normality and identical independent distribution (i.i.d.) of the regression slopes is conducted. The time-series average slope coefficients are divided by their standard errors and multiplied by the square root of the number of observations.

Two sets of regressions are run for each panel, with excess firm value G, as dependent variable: (i) single variable regressions of their current, past and future changes without any control variable, whose results are given in Tables 6.8 and 6.9. And (ii) full variable regressions controlling for the influence of the rest of other variables, as presented in Table 6.10. Only the two-year variable changes are included in the analysis.

We run single level regressions to first evaluate the effects of each variable on the dependent variable independent of influences from any control variable. Following Kothari and Shanken (1992) and Fama and French (1997), we include in each regression a two-year change in future growth opportunities, $\Delta V_{t+2} = (V_{t+2} - V_t)/A_t$, to absorb any noise induced by their unexpected changes. When the dependent variable is G_t, the single-level cross-section regression for R&D, for example, is:

$$G_t = \mu_t + \beta_1 X_t + \beta_2 \Delta X_{t+2} + \beta_3 \Delta X_{t-2} + \beta_4 \Delta V_{t+2} \quad (30)$$

where μ_t is the intercept term, and $\beta_1, \dots, \beta_4$ are regressor coefficients.

Table 6.8 Fama-French Cross-sectional Single Regressions with Excess Value, G_{it} as Dependent Variable

Mean coefficients and their t-statistics from simple regressions run for each year t across all firms. A firm must have data on all variables in the seven-year sample period, 1987–1993. Future change (two-year) in R&D is expressed as: $\Delta X_{t+2} = (X_{t+2} - X_t)/A_t$. Past change (two-year) in R&D is expressed as: $\Delta X_{t-2} = (X_t - X_{t-2})/A_t$. Changes (expected values) in all other variables are computed similarly and scaled as defined in table 6.3, except for L, α, and HH which are ratio changes. Future change (two-year) in market value V_t is expressed as: $\Delta V_{t+2} = (V_{t+2} - V_t)/A_t$. All other variables are as defined in tables 6.3 and 6.6.

Panel A: Emerging Firms

	INT	ET_t	ΔV_{t+2}
Coeff.	2.639	-0.765	-0.147
t (Mean)	4.431	-3.487	-2.516

	INT	A_t	ΔA_{t+2}	ΔA_{t-2}	ΔV_{t+2}
Coeff.	0.405		1.762	0.745	-0.251
t (Mean)	3.647		8.663	2.323	-5.295

	INT	S_t	ΔS_{t+2}	ΔS_{t-2}	ΔV_{t+2}
Coeff.	0.357		1.310	0.271	-0.167
t (Mean)	2.995		8.523	1.068	-3.096

	INT	P_t	ΔP_{t+2}	PP_t	ΔV_{t+2}
Coeff.	0.331	0.023	0.068	-0.005	-0.202
t (Mean)	2.201	0.853	3.261	-0.359	-3.338

	INT	X_t	ΔX_{t+2}	ΔX_{t-2}	ΔV_{t+2}
Coeff.	-0.225	5.148	10.368	3.629	-0.229
t (Mean)	-1.632	6.614	7.610	2.840	-4.229

	INT	Y_t	ΔY_{t+2}	ΔY_{t-2}	ΔV_{t+2}
Coeff.	-0.227	12.695	34.876	-124.2	-0.156
t (Mean)	-0.317	0.797	-0.174	0.184	-2.541

	INT	K_t	ΔK_{t+2}	ΔK_{t-2}	α	ΔV_{t+2}
Coeff.	0.359	3.845	10.438	2.548	-0.172	-0.261
t (Mean)	1.916	1.128	4.277	1.000	-1.566	-4.045

	INT	L_t	ΔL_{t+2}	ΔL_{t-2}	ΔV_{t+2}
Coeff.	0.577	-0.009	0.012	-0.005	-0.107
t (Mean)	1.852	-2.108	4.335	-1.137	-1.820

	INT	D_t	ΔD_{t+2}	ΔD_{t-2}	ΔV_{t+2}
Coeff.	0.605	0.010	0.309	-0.213	-0.218
t (Mean)	3.433	0.114	3.576	-1.221	-3.312

	INT	CF_t	ΔCF_{t+2}	ΔCF_{t-2}	ΔV_{t+2}
Coeff.	0.879	-3.354	0.016	1.203	-0.170
t (Mean)	6.406	-5.837	-0.040	1.944	-2.788

	INT	HH_t	ΔHH_{t+2}	ΔHH_{t-2}	ΔV_{t+2}
Coeff.	1.433	-0.001	0.002	-0.002	-0.156
t (Mean)	0.482	-0.091	0.079	0.260	-2.561

	INT	σ_t	$\Delta \sigma_{t+2}$	$\Delta \sigma_{t-2}$	ΔV_{t+2}
Coeff.	0.086	0.640	0.444	0.021	-0.146
t (Mean)	0.087	1.765	1.320	-0.248	-2.426

Table 6.9 Fama-French Cross-sectional Single Regressions with Excess Value, G_{t}, as Dependent Variable

Mean coefficients and their t-statistics from simple regressions run for each year t across all firms. All variables and their changes are as defined in tables 6.3, 6.6 and 6.8. A firm must have data on all variables in the seven-year sample period, 1987–1993. Future change (two-year) in market value V_t is expressed as: $\Delta V_{t+2} = (V_{t+2} - V_t)/A_t$.

	INT	ET_t			ΔV_{t+2}
Coeff.	1.297	-0.338			0.088
t (Mean)	3.544	-3.818			3.247

	INT		ΔA_{t+2}	ΔA_{t-2}	ΔV_{t+2}
Coeff.	-0.063		0.681	1.032	0.068
t (Mean)	-2.083		2.652	3.026	2.168

	INT		ΔS_{t+2}	ΔS_{t-2}	ΔV_{t+2}
Coeff.	-0.078		0.039	0.729	0.128
t (Mean)	-2.473		-0.880	4.048	4.089

	INT	P_t	ΔP_{t+2}	PP_t	ΔV_{t+2}
Coeff.	0.008	-0.029	0.054	-0.045	0.109
t (Mean)	-1.266	-0.439	1.760	-1.872	3.666

	INT	X_t	ΔX_{t+2}	ΔX_{t-2}	ΔV_{t+2}
Coeff.	-0.121	0.847	5.412	5.918	0.104
t (Mean)	-2.043	0.697	2.265	1.754	3.340

	INT	Y_t	ΔY_{t+2}	ΔY_{t-2}	ΔV_{t+2}
Coeff.	-0.238	3.713	-10.30	10.388	0.103
t (Mean)	-1.852	1.043	-0.157	0.296	3.586

Panel B: Mature Firms

INT	K_t	ΔK_{t+2}	ΔK_{t-2}	α_t	ΔV_{t+2}
-0.315	5.117	8.809	1.752	-0.052	0.055
-3.649	3.582	4.476	0.742	-0.540	2.266

INT	L_t	ΔL_{t+2}	ΔL_{t-2}		ΔV_{t+2}
-0.327	0.011	-0.004	-0.005		0.119
-2.736	3.067	-0.895	-1.856		4.445

INT	D_t	ΔD_{t+2}	ΔD_{t-2}		ΔV_{t+2}
0.034	-0.070	0.006	0.067		0.111
0.064	-1.152	-0.518	0.436		3.680

INT	CF_t	ΔCF_{t+2}	ΔCF_{t-2}		ΔV_{t+2}
-0.679	4.565	1.192	0.495		0.059
-8.494	8.382	1.415	1.147		2.028

INT	HH_t	ΔHH_{t+2}	ΔHH_{t-2}		ΔV_{t+2}
-0.116	0.000	-0.001	0.000		0.109
-2.113	1.463	-0.624	0.554		3.777

INT	σ_t	$\Delta \sigma_{t+2}$	$\Delta \sigma_{t-2}$		ΔV_{t+2}
0.064	-0.170	-0.273	0.133		0.122
0.238	-0.972	-2.001	0.162		4.131

Table 6.10 Fama-MacBeth Cross-sectional Full Regressions with Excess Value, G_t, as Dependent Variable

Mean coefficients and their t-statistics from simple regressions run for each year t across all firms. All variables and their changes are as defined in tables 6.3, 6.6 and 6.8. A firm must have data on all variables in the seven-year sample period, 1987–1993. Future change (two-year) in market value V_t is expressed as: $\Delta V_{t+2} = (V_{t+2} - V_t)/A_t$. t-statistic in parenthesis.

Variable	Emerging Firms	Mature Firms	Variable	Emerging Firms	Mature Firms
INT	9.124	-0.294	α_t	-0.024	0.144
	(0.409)	(-1.114)		(-0.152)	(1.687)
ET_t	-0.392	-0.221	L_t	0.002	0.003
	(2.364)	(-1.998)		(0.512)	(0.702)
ΔA_{t+2}	1.457	0.709	ΔL_{t+2}	-0.001	-0.004
	(4.142)	(0.981)		(-0.240)	(-0.852)
ΔA_{t-2}	2.580	-0.307	ΔL_{t-2}	-0.002	0.003
	(5.125)	(-0.154)		(-0.175)	(0.618)
ΔS_{t+2}	-0.098	-0.503	D_t	-0.026	0.065
	(0.377)	(-2.001)		(-0.220)	(0.894)
ΔS_{t-2}	-0.596	-0.038	ΔD_{t+2}	-0.071	-0.088
	(-1.928)	(-0.138)		(-0.488)	(-0.400)
P_t	-0.009	-0.037	ΔD_{t-2}	-0.643	0.037
	(-0.273)	(-1.448)		(-3.509)	(0.102)
PP_t	0.063	-0.022	CF_t	-3.049	5.914
	(1.295)	(-0.927)		(-4.170)	(6.738)
ΔP_{t+2}	0.010	0.072	ΔCF_{t+2}	-0.621	1.409
	(0.627)	(2.923)		(-1.467)	(1.487)
X_t	4.040	-5.711	ΔCF_{t-2}	0.354	-0.984
	(3.438)	(-4.195)		(0.313)	(-1.282)
ΔX_{t+2}	4.681	-0.559	HH_t	-0.004	0.000
	(2.083)	(-0.884)		(-0.351)	(1.518)
ΔX_{t-2}	0.559	-2.335	ΔHH_{t+2}	-0.018	-0.002
	(0.384)	(-0.852)		(-0.960)	(-1.324)
Y_t	-45.734	-3.729	ΔHH_{t-2}	0.001	0.000
	(-0.435)	(-0.061)		(-0.138)	(0.571)
ΔY_{t+2}	18.382	19.759	σ_t	0.180	0.271
	(-1.209)	(0.810)		(0.649)	(1.141)
ΔY_{t-2}	18.504	60.109	$\Delta \sigma_{t+2}$	0.507	0.358
	(0.628)	(0.860)		(2.217)	(2.014)
K_t	-3.053	1.873	$\Delta \sigma_{t-2}$	0.301	0.231
	(-1.386)	(1.104)		(1.299)	(1.456)
ΔK_{t+2}	0.014	1.824	ΔV_{t+2}	-0.264	0.035
	(0.141)	(0.928)		(-4.583)	(1.168)
ΔK_{t-2}	-0.794	4.030			
	(-0.269)	(1.904)			

We then conduct a full level regression analysis to determine if each of the variables would still retain its power in explaining changes in growth opportunities, after controlling for all other variables including the noise term. We examine if the coefficients are not zero and their t-values to confirm our earlier results. The full-level regression is expressed as follows:

$$G_t = \mu_t + \beta_1 ET_t + \beta_2 \Delta A_{t+2} + \beta_3 \Delta A_{t-2} + \beta_4 \Delta S_{t+2} + \beta_5 \Delta S_{t-2}$$

$$+ \beta_6 P_t + \beta_7 \Delta P_{t+2} + \beta_8 PP_t + \beta_9 X_t + \beta_{10} \Delta X_{t+2} + \beta_{11} \Delta X_{t-2}$$

$$+ \beta_{12} Y_t + \beta_{13} \Delta Y_{t+2} + \beta_{14} \Delta Y_{t-2} + \beta_{15} K_t + \beta_{16} \Delta K_{t+2} + \beta_{17} \Delta K_{t-2}$$

$$+ \beta_{18} \alpha_t + \beta_{19} L + \beta_{20} \Delta L_{t+2} + \beta_{21} \Delta L_{t-2} + \beta_{22} D_t + \beta_{23} \Delta D_{t+2}$$

$$+ \beta_{24} \Delta D_{t-2} + \beta_{25} CF_t + \beta_{26} \Delta CF_{t+2} + \beta_{27} \Delta CF_{t-2} + \beta_{28} HH_t$$

$$+ \beta_{29} \Delta HH_{t+2} + \beta_{30} \Delta HH_{t-2} + \beta_{31} \sigma_t + \beta_{32} \Delta \sigma_{t+2} + \beta_{33} \Delta \sigma_{t-2}$$

$$+ \beta_{34} \Delta V_{t+2} \tag{31}$$

For emerging firms, the net investment components of internal capital (ΔA_{t+2} and ΔA_{t-2}) are positive and significantly different from zero, with t-values between 2.323 and 8.663 standard errors above zero in the single regressions in Table 6.8. In the full regression in Table 6.10, these variables still retain their power when subjected to control variables, with standard errors of 4.142 and 5.125 above zero. The past change in operating cash flows (ΔCF_{t-2}) is positive, with a t-value of 1.944 standard errors above zero in the single regression although in the full regression it loses its power. Current operating cash flow (CF_t) remains significantly negative with t-values of −5.837 and −4.170 standard errors above zero in the single and full regressions, respectively. The expected future change (ΔCF_{t+2}), however, has a weak and mixed influence. These results are very consistent with the findings in Table 6.4. There is thus, strong evidence that internal capital significantly influences growth opportunities of emerging firms.

As for established companies, net investments are positive and significant in the single regressions in Table 6.9. However, when controlled for other variables in the full regression, they become less influential and, in fact, show a change of sign (Table 6.10). Overall, net investment explains changes in growth opportunities more in emerging firms than it does in mature firms. Operating cash flows are positive in both regressions (except past change), and current value is highly significant. This again confirms our results in tables 6.5.

Table 6.8 indicates that R&D variables of emerging firms (X_t, ΔX_{t+2} and ΔX_{t-2}) significantly contributes to changes in growth opportunities. When controlled (Table 6.10), they lose some power except current R&D (X_t) which remains significantly positive. These contrast with mature firms whose R&D variables in the single regression are positive, but not as significant and the current R&D in the full regression is significantly negative.

Rival R&D has some effect on the dependent variable though not significant. There is evidence that past change in rival R&D (ΔY_{t-2}) has a positive influence but current level (Y_t) and future change (ΔY_{t+2}) have negative effects on growth opportunities of emerging firms (Table 6.10). Independent of control variables, however, current rival R&D show a positive effect. For mature firms, rival R&D are not significant but they bear influence nevertheless. In the single regression, current and past rival R&D are positive but in the full regression, current rival R&D are negative while past and future changes are positive. We can conclude that for both mature and emerging firms, current rival R&D is beneficial. But when controlled for other variables, they show a negative relationship and only past change show a positive effect.

In the single regression, current patents (P_t) are positive, future change in patents (ΔP_{t+2}) is positive and significant, and stock of patents (PP_t) is negative for emerging firms. When controlled for other influences, current patents lose power and become negative, future changes in patents lose power but remain positive and stock of patents gains power and become positive. For mature firms, expected change in patents remains positive and significant whereas current and past change in patents are negative, with less influence in the control regression.

All current (K_t), past (ΔK_{t-2}) and future (ΔK_{t+2}) changes in capital expenditures for mature firms are positive. Current and future change variables show significance in the single regression but only past change in capital expenditure is significant after controlling for other influences. For emerging firms, only future changes in capital expenditure show a positive relationship in the full regression. In terms of volatility in capital expenditures (α_t), the coefficient for emerging firms is negative in both single and full regressions. It is negative in the single regression but becomes positive in the full regression for mature firms. Nevertheless, it still lends support to the prediction of the model.

There is evidence that debt has a significantly negative relationship with changes in growth opportunities for emerging firms. This is not the same for mature firms which show that only future changes in debt (ΔD_{t+2}) is negative but current (D_t) and past debt (ΔD_{t-2}) levels are positive though not significant (Table 6.10).

Another important factor to determine is the effect of volatility of the investment project (σ_t). The results indicate that volatility has a positive effect on growth opportunities for both subsamples. Future volatility ($\Delta\sigma_{t+2}$) has a particularly stronger effect for emerging firms whereas for mature firms it is past volatility ($\Delta\sigma_{t-2}$) which is significant. The prediction of the model that volatility of the project should contribute positively to the change in real growth option is thus supported.

Growth in sales (ΔS_{t+2} and ΔS_{t-2}) which are meant to proxy expected benefits of monopoly rents are positive and significant in the single regression for emerging firms as expected. However, they lose power drastically in the full regression, showing negative coefficients. The picture is similar for mature firms. The Herfindahl-Herschman index (HH) shows very little influence in both panels.

Following Fama and French (1997), we run regressions of only the change parameters on change value of growth opportunities, $\Delta G_t = [(V_t - A_t) - (V_{t-2} - A_{t-2})]/A_t$. This is an alternative technique to the common event-study methodology and has the advantage of measuring valuation effects on a longer-term than the event studies do. The change-cross-section regressions are similarly expressed as in Equation 30 for single-level and in Equation 30 for full-level, with the exception that only change variables are included. All current variables are omitted. The results, presented in Tables 6.11, 6.12 and 6.13 are still very consistent with earlier analysis.

6.4 CONCLUSION

The empirical study examines the determinants of growth opportunities, particularly the relevant variables that spawn the real

Table 6.11 Fama-French Cross-sectional Single Regressions with Change in Excess Value, $\Delta G_t = [(V_t - A_t) - (V_{t-2} - A_{t-2})]/A_t$, as Dependent Variable

Mean coefficients and their t-statistics from simple regressions run for each year t across all firms. A firm must have data on all variables in the seven-year sample period, 1987–1993. Future change (two-year) in market value V_t is expressed as: $\Delta V_{t+2}=(V_{t+2} - V_t)/A_t$. All other variables are as defined in tables 6.3, 6.6 and 6.8.

Panel A: Emerging Firms

	INT	ET$_t$		ΔV$_{t+2}$
Coeff.	-0.430	0.224		-0.230
t (Mean)	-0.926	1.324		-4.804

	INT	ΔK$_{t+2}$	ΔK$_{t-2}$	α$_t$	ΔV$_{t+2}$
Coeff.	0.186	4.039	1.654	-0.159	-0.308
t (Mean)	1.485	2.500	0.852	-2.231	-6.045

	INT	ΔA$_{t+2}$	ΔA$_{t-2}$	ΔV$_{t+2}$
Coeff.	0.047	1.155	0.017	-0.348
t (Mean)	0.545	8.736	-0.501	-9.151

	INT	ΔI$_{t+2}$	ΔI$_{t-2}$	ΔV$_{t+2}$
Coeff.	0.332	0.003	-0.006	-0.222
t (Mean)	1.455	1.376	-2.609	-4.979

	INT	ΔS$_{t+2}$	ΔS$_{t-2}$	ΔV$_{t+2}$
Coeff.	0.088	0.503	-0.202	-0.230
t (Mean)	0.810	4.960	-1.663	-5.527

	INT	ΔD$_{t+2}$	ΔD$_{t-2}$	ΔV$_{t+2}$
Coeff.	0.191	-0.025	-0.273	-0.280
t (Mean)	1.461	0.800	-2.211	-5.665

	INT	ΔP$_{t+2}$	ΔP$_{t-2}$	ΔV$_{t+2}$
Coeff.	0.202	-0.002	-0.001	-0.279
t (Mean)	1.576	-0.749	0.453	-5.976

	INT	ΔCF$_{t+2}$	ΔCF$_{t-2}$	ΔV$_{t+2}$
Coeff.	0.173	0.017	0.029	-0.246
t (Mean)	1.345	-0.835	0.774	-4.702

	INT	ΔX$_{t+2}$	ΔX$_{t-2}$	ΔV$_{t+2}$
Coeff.	0.092	4.535	0.469	-0.259
t (Mean)	0.902	4.576	0.179	-5.984

	INT	ΔHH$_{t+2}$	ΔHH$_{t-2}$	ΔV$_{t+2}$
Coeff.	0.251	0.001	0.001	-0.357
t (Mean)	1.707	1.026	0.307	-5.300

	INT	ΔY$_{t+2}$	ΔY$_{t-2}$	ΔV$_{t+2}$
Coeff.	0.105	-3.766	7.696	-0.253
t (Mean)	0.446	-0.070	0.723	-5.303

	INT	Δσ$_{t+2}$	Δσ$_{t-2}$	ΔV$_{t+2}$
Coeff.	0.251	0.053	0.179	-0.246
t (Mean)	1.707	0.176	0.658	-4.702

option and their implications for both emerging and mature firms. As predicted, the empirical results demonstrate that the magnitudes of growth opportunities of emerging and established firms are significantly different. On average, 63 percent of the market value of an emerging firm is accounted for by growth opportunities compared with only 7 percent for a mature firm. We recognize that all the firms in our sample are followed by Compustat, and may have already been qualified as "successful" with "tractable" performance of existing assets. It is therefore conceivable that the contribution of intangible growth options to the market value could be much higher than reported for emerging firms.

Table 6.12 Fama-French Cross-sectional Single Regressions with Change in Excess Value, $\Delta G_t = [(V_t - A_t)-(V_{t-2}-A_{t-2})]/A_t$, as Dependent Variable

Mean coefficients and their t-statistics from simple regressions run for each year t across all firms. All variables and their changes are as defined in tables 6.3, 6.6 and 6.8. A firm must have data on all variables in the seven-year sample period, 1987–1993. Future change (two-year) in market value V_t is expressed as: $\Delta V_{t+2} = (V_{t+2} - V_t)/A_t$.

Panel B: Mature Firms

	INT	ET_t		ΔV_{t+2}
Coeff.	0.478	-0.125		0.048
t (Mean)	1.206	-1.439		2.183

	INT	ΔK_{t+2}	ΔK_{t-2}	α_t	ΔV_{t+2}
Coeff.	-0.017	5.082	1.388	-0.072	0.019
t (Mean)	-1.353	3.905	1.169	-1.294	0.867

	INT	ΔA_{t+2}	ΔA_{t-2}	ΔV_{t+2}
Coeff.	-0.055	0.424	0.321	0.022
t (Mean)	-2.401	2.781	1.609	0.869

	INT	ΔL_{t+2}	ΔL_{t-2}	ΔV_{t+2}
Coeff.	-0.063	0.005	-0.006	0.047
t (Mean)	-1.367	3.896	-3.704	2.220

	INT	ΔS_{t+2}	ΔS_{t-2}	ΔV_{t+2}
Coeff.	-0.056	0.008	0.560	0.049
t (Mean)	-2.621	0.080	2.653	2.080

	INT	ΔD_{t+2}	ΔD_{t-2}	ΔV_{t+2}
Coeff.	-0.014	0.020	0.024	0.056
t (Mean)	-1.523	-0.192	0.326	2.467

	INT	ΔP_{t+2}	ΔP_{t-2}	ΔV_{t+2}
Coeff.	-0.010	0.026	-0.025	0.051
t (Mean)	-1.221	2.660	-2.997	2.201

	INT	ΔCF_{t+2}	ΔCF_{t-2}	ΔV_{t+2}
Coeff.	-0.024	0.677	2.766	0.016
t (Mean)	-1.993	1.792	8.214	0.672

	INT	ΔX_{t+2}	ΔX_{t-2}	ΔV_{t+2}
Coeff.	-0.035	4.106	0.526	0.043
t (Mean)	-1.959	2.823	0.390	1.734

	INT	ΔHH_{t+2}	ΔHH_{t-2}	ΔV_{t+2}
Coeff.	-0.003	0.000	0.000	0.055
t (Mean)	-1.474	0.609	-0.931	2.431

	INT	ΔY_{t+2}	ΔY_{t-2}	ΔV_{t+2}
Coeff.	-0.013	-11.75	16.978	0.050
t (Mean)	-0.703	-1.264	1.440	2.125

	INT	Δσ_{t+2}	Δσ_{t-2}	ΔV_{t+2}
Coeff.	-0.042	-0.259	-0.023	0.064
t (Mean)	-1.641	-2.576	-0.729	2.778

Based on the theoretical model, we hypothesize that emerging firms tend to rely more on internal capital as opposed to mature companies that have greater access to external capital markets to finance investment opportunities. This is strongly supported by the empirical results. For emerging firms, R&D expenditures are significantly positive and internal capital markets are significant negative. These results are consistent with our model in the sense that internal cash flows are expected to be exhausted in financing innovation, with R&D being a valuable determinant of growth opportunities since it serves to speed up innovation and shorten the maturity date of the real call option.

Table 6.13 Fama-MacBeth Cross-sectional Full Regressions with Change in Excess Value, $\Delta G_t = [(V_t - A_t) - (V_{t-2} - A_{t-2})]/A_t$, as Dependent Variable

Mean coefficients and their t-statistics from simple regressions run for each year t across all firms. All variables and their changes are as defined in tables 6.3, 6.6 and 6.8. A firm must have data on all variables in the seven-year sample period, 1987–1993. Future change (two-year) in market value V_t is expressed as: $\Delta V_{t+2} = (V_{t+2} - V_t)/A_t$. t-statistic in parenthesis.

Variable	Emerging Firms	Mature Firms	Variable	Emerging Firms	Mature Firms
INT	-0.485	0.084	ΔK_{t-2}	-1.549	1.928
	(-0.512)	(-0.174)		(-0.830)	(1.312)
ET_t	0.204	-0.071	α_t	-0.160	-0.026
	(1.207)	(-0.611)		(-2.481)	(-0.637)
ΔA_{t+2}	1.250	0.419	ΔL_{t+2}	0.001	0.001
	(4.933)	(0.457)		(0.267)	(1.057)
ΔA_{t-2}	0.680	-0.298	ΔL_{t-2}	-0.002	-0.001
	(1.679)	(-1.420)		(-1.252)	(-0.403)
ΔS_{t+2}	0.090	-0.268	ΔD_{t+2}	-0.082	-0.062
	(0.256)	(-1.660)		(-0.619)	(-1.176)
ΔS_{t-2}	-0.784	0.047	ΔD_{t-2}	-0.129	0.029
	(-2.590)	(-0.433)		(-1.037)	(0.572)
ΔP_{t+2}	-0.009	0.035	ΔCF_{t+2}	-1.041	0.599
	(-0.496)	(3.305)		(-1.573)	(1.075)
ΔP_{t-2}	0.010	-0.024	ΔCF_{t-2}	0.983	2.383
	(1.191)	(-2.997)		(1.855)	(4.505)
ΔX_{t+2}	1.496	-1.051	ΔHH_{t+2}	0.002	0.000
	(1.178)	(-0.769)		(0.337)	(-0.550)
ΔX_{t-2}	2.544	-3.515	ΔHH_{t-2}	- 0.001	0.000
	(1.881)	(-1.906)		(-0.165)	(-0.682)
ΔY_{t+2}	-30.805	2.334	$\Delta \sigma_{t+2}$	-0.018	-0.083
	(-0.547)	(0.300)		(-0.025)	(-0.526)
ΔY_{t-2}	30.805	5.845	$\Delta \sigma_{t-2}$	0.331	0.245
	(0.212)	(0.316)		(1.775)	(1.972)
ΔK_{t+2}	1.875	2.136	ΔV_{t+2}	-0.385	-0.001
	(1.057)	(1.628)		(-7.253)	(-0.180)

However, mature firms show the opposite results: internal cash flows have a positive and significant influence on growth opportunities while R&D is negative and significant. A plausible explanation is that the market recognizes available investment opportunity sets for these firms but may prefer that they purchase ready technology through, for instance, synergistic mergers and acquisitions rather than engaging in risky R&D investments which have very uncertain payoffs.

If growth opportunities were a significant component of the market value of emerging firms, then we would expect acquisition of debt to have a negative impact due to the under-investment hypothesis of Myers (1977). We document that emerging firms have lower debt ratio than mature firms, but this difference is not significant. We also find that debt is negative for emerging firms but positive for mature firms. However, these influences are not significant, further indicating a weaker support for the hypothesis. As explained earlier, the emerging firms in our sample may not be "unknowns" in the market after all. Thus, they don't suffer from the capital markets constraints to the extent that a typical start-up firm would.

Patents are predicted by the model to be a good proxy for the time to maturity of the real option. Thus, we would expect patents to have a positive influence on growth opportunities. Our results show that they are valuable. However, they tend to lose power when controlled for other variables, especially R&D. Nevertheless, past patents and R&D have significantly positive impact on the output of current patents.

We also find that volatility in capital expenditures has a negative influence on emerging firms but a positive effect on mature firms, as predicted. However, their effects are not significant. The capital expenditure levels, except past changes, show a week and negative influence on growth opportunities for emerging firms but a strong positive correlation for mature firms. These results support the model prediction, and indicate that capital expenditures are a necessary price to pay to acquire the monopoly rents. However, the unexpected variation in the level of the strike price may lead to possibility of a firm leaving the real option unexercised, thereby foregoing the benefits of innovation. The positive effect for mature firms tends to suggest that they are well diversified and have adequate hedging possibilities.

The riskier the R&D investments, the more valuable the real growth option, strongly supporting the prediction of the model. However, this effect is weaker for mature firms, perhaps due to their ability to diversify, and the fact that their investments may be supported more by existing assets (collateral effect).

NOTES

1. See Millman, Joel, October 12, 1998, "Mexican Companies Scale Back Expansion Plans as Growth Prospects in Latin America Diminish." *The Wall Street Journal.*

2. Some researchers have only looked at the investment variables like R&D (Morbey (1989), Morbey and Reithner (1990), Shevlin (1991), Hall (1993)); R&D and patents (Griliches (1981), Bound, Cummins, Griliches, Hall, and Adam (1984), Ben-Zion (1984), Jaffe (1986), Cockburn and Griliches (1988), Austin (1993), Megna and Klock (1993)); or advertising and R&D (Lustgarten and Thomadakis (1987), Morck and Yeung (1991), Chauvin and Hirschey (1993)). Others have explored financing and the effects of risk (Chung and Charoenwong (1991)); risk and market structure (Thomadakis (1977)); and capital expenditures (McConnell and Muscarella (1985), Beranek, Cornwell and Choi (1995)).

3. Including Austin (1993), and Megna and Klock (1993).

4. Related work that have applied event-studies methodology include McConnell and Muscarella (1985), Chan, Martin and Kensinger (1990), Szewczyk, Tsetsekos, and Zantout (1996), and Blose and Shieh (1997).

5. Until 1995, an inventor in the United States had exclusive right to a patent for 17 years.

6. The patent data were hand collected.

7. Gompers (1995) documents a surge in venture capital financing in the U.S. throughout the 1980s and 1990s which may have been a critical catalyst for funding emerging firms and introducing them to the capital markets. Compared to other financial markets, the U.S. is the most efficient and liquid. The U.S. stock markets, especially the Initial Public Offerings (IPOs), have recorded substantial growth in the last 10 to 15 years. Also, see *Business Week,* August 18, 1997.

CHAPTER 7

Summary, Problems and Future Research

"I still can't make the math correlate with the stock prices."
–Lise Buyer, CS First Boston.[1]

7.1 Summary

7.1.1 Valuing Growth Opportunities

For many companies, the value of growth opportunities is greater than the value of assets-in-place. This is particularly true for start-up and emerging firms, although it may not be so important for well-established firms. The possibility that current investments may influence future opportunities, either by creating growth opportunities or minimizing the value of an existing opportunity set is widely accepted. However, despite known potentials, the scope of actual economic interactions of current options and future corporate growth opportunities have been far less understood. Traditional valuation techniques have tended to ignore the qualitative difference between real growth options and the assets-in-place and such strategic values due to financing, investing and operating flexibilities are never measured.

Whereas this problem may have limited implications for mature firms, it is critical for start-up ventures where the bulk of market value is in the intangible investment opportunities. These intangible assets are real options whose valuation is the focus of this book. The central point in this investigation is the recognition that firms are not endowed with real growth options. This implies that the issue of how real options are distributed among firms becomes nontrivial.

We have developed a model for valuing growth opportunities of a firm that is internally generated. The model begins with the allocation of real growth options through competitive investments in basic R&D and formulates valuation of growth opportunities as compound real options. The process starts with a firm having an original idea for making a breakthrough discovery and introducing a new product into the market. That idea must be financed, through R&D investments, and the discovery made sooner otherwise a successful competitor may overtake the firm and win. A firm that loses the competitive race to innovate gets zero value of growth opportunities.

Once a discovery is made, the successful firm must decide to make additional investments to manufacture the product. Thus, R&D is essentially a real call option. The underlying asset is the expected value of a completed investment project. Maturity date is the time the discovery is made and the firm simultaneously decides whether to produce. The exercise price is the manufacturing expenditure, which is considered uncertain as the R&D investments proceed. Volatility of the underlying asset comes from the risk of the expected cash flows from a completed project as well as the uncertainty surrounding the capital investment.

Sometimes mass-producing a breakthrough product may not be sufficient. Additional investments in advertising and marketing may be required to open up the market for the new product. The firm can only choose to incur advertising costs if the enhanced value it generates consequently is greater than the value it would have earned without making this additional expenditure. We therefore model advertising investment as a real exchange option where the original project value is the delivery asset and the enhanced value received is the option asset. In sum, the value of internally generated growth opportunities is modeled as a combination of a real call option and an exchange option.

There are essentially five components of this investigation. First, the theoretical model is developed. Second, qualitative comparative analysis is carried out to determine the direction of change of the explanatory variables with respect to the exogenous variable. Third, a scenario analysis is conducted to examine the impact of each of the variables identified in the model on the value of growth opportunities. Fourth, a binomial option pricing approach is applied to explore the financing options of a growth project. Finally, real data on a sample of firms is analyzed to test the model and identify any deviations from the theoretical and scenario analysis results, and compare with earlier findings in existing finance literature.

7.1.2 Internal Capital Markets and Growth Opportunities

Because of information asymmetry surrounding basic R&D investments, access to internal sources of financing is a binding constraint on emerging firms. The theoretical model implies that internal cash flow should have a greater effect on growth opportunities for these firms. The empirical analysis documents evidence that emerging firms tend to rely more on internal capital as opposed to mature companies that have greater access to the capital markets for external funding. This is consistent with Lamont (1997) who finds that decreases in cash flow decrease investments, and Myers and Majluf's information asymmetry model (1984) which implies that a decline in internal finance introduces under-investment problem. Fazzari, Hubbard, and Peterson (1988), and Hoshi, Kashyap, and Scharfstein (1991) also provide evidence that investment is related to the availability of internal funds.

7.1.3 Leverage and Growth Opportunities

We find that debt has a negative contribution to growth opportunities for emerging firms, albeit a weak result, consistent with the tradition of Myers (1977) suggesting that a firm's borrowing should be inversely related to the extent that its value depends on the value of future investment opportunities. These results are in contrast with Lang, Ofek, and Stulz (1996) who find that there is a negative relation between leverage and growth only for firms with low Tobin's Q. A liquidity argument to the debt over-hang hypothesis is that leverage should reduce growth more for firms with valuable growth opportunities, because such firms have greater informational asymmetries, making external funds more expensive to obtain. The agency costs of managerial discretion (Jensen 1986, Stulz 1990) also imply that the adverse impact on leverage on growth increases firm value by preventing managers from taking poor projects.

We establish contradictory results for mature firms. They exhibit a positive correlation of debt ratio with growth opportunities, although the effect is not significant. One could explain this behavior in the context of Schlingemann (1998) that, if management has exhausted all positive NPV projects, the likelihood of investing in negative NPV projects increases with greater levels of managerial discretion over investment funds. Thus, the choice of debt financing, which lowers managerial discretion, merely signals that the market recognizes ample positive NPV projects available for well established firms.

Our results also show that emerging firms have lower debt ratio than mature firms, although this difference is not significant. They provide support to existing capital structure literature indicating that managers of firms with valuable growth opportunities should choose lower leverage because these companies might not be able to take advantage of their investment opportunities if they have to raise outside funds. Smith and Watts (1992), and Jung, Kim, and Stulz (1995) also provide supportive evidence that firms with valuable growth opportunities choose low leverage. Myers (1977) shows that the amount of debt supported by growth opportunities will be less, other things equal, than is supported by assets already in place. Mackie-Mason (1990) also finds that firms that have exhausted their tax shields (i.e., have little or no taxable income) are less likely to choose debt financing.

7.1.4 R&D and Rival R&D

The critical role of R&D expenditure of the firm and of its rival in the model is to speed up innovation and shorten the maturity date of the real call option. R&D (and to some extent past R&D) generally has a significant influence on innovation, and a strong positive correlation with growth opportunities of emerging firms. These findings are consistent with Bound et al (1984), Cockburn and Griliches (1988), Megna and Klock (1993), Chauvin and Hirschey (1993), and Szewczyk, Tsetsekos, and Zantout (1996). In contrast, we find that R&D of mature firms, when controlled for other variables show a negative relation with growth opportunities. Here is a plausible explanation. Given that the market has recognized available growth opportunity sets for these firms, the agency cost of managerial discretion (Stulz 1990) and the over-investment problem of free cash flow of Jensen (1986) imply that investing in the more risky basic R&D, with uncertain payoff, is considered wasteful.

Rival R&D is beneficial to the extent that it lowers the expected time of successfully completing R&D project. Jaffe (1986) suggests that rival R&D spillovers constitute a positive externality. Our model results show that the benefit from rival R&D is overshadowed by its negative effect on the profits of the firm due to competition, in line with Ben-Zion (1984) and Jaffe (1986). Expected future values of rival R&D have especially negative impact on growth opportunities and reflects the confounding negative effect of competition.

7.1.5 Patents

The valuation of patents has often generated mixed results and controversies. Recently, with the emergence of biotechnology industry, the issue picked up renewed interest. Hamilton (1996) argues that calculations of quantity rather than quality are worthless, citing Japan's Takeda Chemical Industries Ltd. that was ranked first among biotech corporate patent holders in Europe, Japan and the U.S. but hasn't developed any gene-related drug. Other studies have shown that the usefulness of patents may be industry-related. Ben-Zion (1984) explains that not all patents result in the production of a new profitable product. However, a firm's patents are relevant for other firms in the industry in the sense that they contribute to increased technical knowledge or indicate a potential for new lines of research.

Griliches (1981) suggests that both R&D and patents are inputs of innovation. Cockburn and Griliches (1988) find that in the absence of R&D variables, past patents are significantly valuable. Austin (1993) shows that patents are useful as indicators of innovative output and may produce no value if they have been fully anticipated by the market. Our results establish that patents are valuable, and have a significant influence on innovation. When controlled for other variables, however, only past stock of patents for emerging firms retain power whereas it is the expected future patents that are valuable for established firms. Subject to industry performance, a firm's patents can be a good proxy for the time to maturity of the real options.

7.1.6 Capital Expenditure

One key parameter of our model is the magnitude of the strike price, the capital investment, which is critical in determining the exercise decision of the firm. Because of the uncertainty underlying the process of innovation, the actual amount to be paid as the exercise price, may be unknown at the time the discovery is made. If it turns out that the required capital investment is too high, the option is not exercised and the growth opportunities are lost.

We find that capital expenditure has a negative influence on growth opportunities for emerging firms but a positive effect for mature firms. Existing research, for instance, Pindyck (1993), Beranek, Cornwell, and Choi (1995), and Blose and Shieh (1997) have examined the effect of capital expenditure only on capital projects or mature firms. Although they document evidence similar to our findings for established firms, the distinction with relatively young companies is not considered. The emerging firms' sample contrasts these existing results and strongly supports the prediction of our model.

We document that volatility in capital expenditures has a negative impact on emerging firms, implying that the high volatility may lead to an increased amount of required capital spending to the extent that the growth option is not worth exercising. This may be explained in part by Fazzari et al (1988) who provide evidence that when firms rely heavily on internal funds for financing investments, their expenditures on investments are more sensitive to fluctuations in cash flows than high-dividend-paying firms.

Consistent with our results for mature firms, McConnel and Muscarella (1985) also find that unanticipated increases in planned capital expenditures have a positive effect on the market value of the firm, and that unanticipated decreases have a negative effect. The implication is that for well-established firms that have more access to the capital markets, the opportunity cost of passing up a valuable investment opportunity far exceeds the cost of hedging the uncertainty in capital investment.

7.1.7 Monopoly Rents and Underlying Risk

We have shown that the expected benefit to be derived from a successfully completed R&D investment is positively related to the real growth option, consistent with the prediction of option pricing theory. Emerging firms are found to be significantly riskier than well established firms, supporting Chung and Chareonwang (1991) who conclude that a firm that has large portion of its value accounted for by the present value of future growth opportunities, would exhibit a higher stock risk than the mature firm whose value is largely determined by the capitalized value of an earnings stream generated by existing assets. Furthermore, we find that the riskier the monopoly rents the more valuable the real growth option. This effect is strong for emerging firms but weak for mature firms, given the low volatility of the latter due to their very diversified nature.

7.2 Data and Sample Selection Problems

As in many empirical investigations, this study has encountered lack of ample data set to test the model. This problem is particularly true for young and emerging firms, which are the main focus of the model.

For a firm to qualify to be included in the sample it must be a U.S. publicly traded company, tracked by Compustat, have non-missing data for all relevant variables from 1987 to 1993, be covered by CASSIS CD-ROM (for patents) during the period 1969–1993, and belong to the Standard Industrial Classification code 3000 (manufacturing). These specifications effectively reduced the sample size considerably from a potential 1,000 to the final 208 firms. Furthermore, since companies followed by Compustat are reasonably successful, some young struggling firms may have been excluded, introducing a survivorship bias in the analysis.

There may be also problems associated with the construction of the variables. Patent count, for instance, is the only variable used to proxy for innovation timing, yet there is evidence that such measures as citation impact, cycle time, and science links are valuable indicators of a firm's potential to succeed in making a breakthrough discovery. It was not possible to gather these data for our samples. Also, some of the variables that appear redundant may be omitted.

Another problem concerns what may be considered "standard" or "more acceptable" definition and classification of "emerging firm" or "growth firm." Our criterion was determined by dividend payments policy, based on evidence from signaling theory and capital markets constraints. We classified a firm as "emerging" if it has never issued any dividends since its incorporation, as in Pilotte (1992). Some researchers and practitioners have used price-earnings relationship, market-to-book ratio, and Tobin's q ratio. One may also argue that the growth phenomenon is cyclical citing, for instance, IBM, which has been a mature company but turned into a "growth firm" in the 1990s. And yet another might wonder if Microsoft (which has not paid common dividends) is still emerging.

7.3 Determining Parameter Values

Our valuation model has identified growth opportunities as a function of the speed of innovation, competition, risk, market potential, capital expenditure, volatility in capital expenditure and the cost of hedging it, advertising expenditure, and interest rates. Empirical work in financial economics is the reference point in understanding how these variables are measured in practice. One variable that is critical to our model and, deserves mentioning, is the speed of innovation. There is growing interest empirically in knowing what determines the probability of success of a firm engaged in R&D (See Deng, Lev and Narin (1999)). We list below some of the measures being attempted or used to evaluate corporate R&D performance:

(a)   How often the firm's work is cited in other scientists' work.
(b)   Science link, a measure of the number of references to scientific journals or conference proceedings cited on the patent.
(c)   How many patents are filed or assigned.
(d)   Evaluating a list of research projects and scoring what proportion of all projects pass the test of commercial possibilities.
(e)   Citation impact, a count of the citations received by a company's patent from later patents.
(f)   Cycle time, measures how quickly technology is evolving with respect to the firm's patenting time.
(g)   R&D expenditures and R&D intensity.

These measures may be industry dependent. Some are forward looking while others are backward looking. We still face a challenge in establishing an accurate yardstick, and more work needs to be done to build some form of consensus.

7.4 Future Research

This book suggests several possible avenues for future research, including:

(a) An extension of the empirical work to cover more U.S. firms and industries.

(b) Comparative analysis of determinants of growth opportunities and capital structure of firms in Japan, Western Europe and the U.S. (developed capital markets).

(c) Analysis of determinants of growth opportunities and capital structure of firms in developing and emerging markets, examining the impact of the degree of capital markets development.

(d) Valuation of IPOs and start-up firms (bank, venture capital, and market financing), as well as stages of new product development.

(e) Valuation of advertising expenditure as a real exchange option, with particular reference to new product developments.

(f) Valuation of biotech firms as well as new technology licensing agreements.

(g) Mergers and acquisitions, and diversification strategies.

(h) Privatization and restructuring.

(i) Corporate control: why do firms remain private *vs* why do firms go public?

7.5 Concluding Remarks

We have presented a valuation model for pricing a firm that may have no existing assets as a compound option. Based on the scenario and empirical analyses, the model appears to fit startup and emerging firms especially well. We find that any investment or financing policy that ignores the qualitative difference between real growth options and the assets-in-place is erroneous. In pursuit of innovative breakthroughs and new product developments, consideration of the volatility in capital investment is important, and could even be more so in less developed capital markets.

The model developed here could be further improved. Practitioners would find it to be a very valuable valuation model if the path to determining the parameter values can be smoothed.

NOTE

1. *Fortune*, June 7, 1999, page 78.

Appendix

***Appendix I*: Expected Time of Innovation for a Monopolist**

The expectations of this random variable can be derived by applying the procedure of integration by parts as follows: Let

$$F_{\tau(X)}(\tau(X)) = F(\tau(X)) = \text{Prob}(\tau(X)) \le t) = 1 - e^{-f(X)}$$

$$\Rightarrow f_{\tau(X)}(\tau(X)) = f(\tau(X)) = F'(\tau(X)) = f(X)e^{-f(X)t}$$

$$\Rightarrow E(\tau(X)) = \int_0^\infty \tau f(X)e^{-f(X)t}d\tau = \int_0^\infty v\,du. \text{ Let } v = \tau$$

and $du = f(X)e^{-f(X)t}d\tau$, implying $u = -e^{-f(X)t}$. Therefore,

$$E(\tau(X)) = \int_0^\infty \tau f(X)e^{-f(X)t}d\tau = [-\tau e^{-f(X)t}]_0^\infty + \int_0^\infty e^{-f(X)t}d\tau$$

$$= [-\tau e^{-f(X)t}]_0^\infty + \left[-\frac{1}{f(X)}e^{-f(X)t} \right]_0^\infty$$

$$= [-\tau e^{-f(X)t}]_0^\infty + \left[-\frac{1}{f(X)}e^{-f(X)t} + \frac{1}{f(X)} \right]_0^\infty = 0 + 0 + \frac{1}{f(X)} = \frac{1}{f(X)}$$

Appendix II: Conditional Probability of Innovation

Let $X_H = \tau_H(X_H) \sim \exp(\pi = f(X_H))$, and

$$X_L = \tau_L(X_L) \sim \exp(\lambda = f(X_L)).$$

$$\therefore Prob(X_H \leq X_L \wedge t) = \int_0^t Prob(X_H \leq X_L) dF(X_L)$$

$$+ Prob(X_L > t).Prob(X_L \leq t)$$

$$= \int_0^t (1 - e^{-Xy})\lambda e^{-\lambda y} dy + e^{-\lambda t}[1 - e^{-Xt}] \quad = 1 - e^{-\lambda t}$$

$$-\left(\frac{\lambda}{\lambda + \pi}\right)(1 - e^{-(\lambda + X)}) + e^{-\lambda t} - e^{-(\lambda + X)t}$$

$$= (1 - e^{-(\lambda + \pi)t}) - \left(\frac{\lambda}{\lambda + \pi}\right)(1 - e^{-(\lambda + X)}) =$$

$$\left(1 - \frac{\lambda}{\lambda + \pi}\right)(1 - e^{-(\lambda + X)})$$

$$= \left(\frac{\pi}{\lambda + \pi}\right)(1 - e^{-(\lambda + X)}) = \left(\frac{f(X_H)}{f(X_L) + f(X_H)}\right)(1 - e^{-t[f(X_L) + f(X_H)]})$$

Appendix III: Expected Time of Innovation for a Doupolist

To determine the value of t, we know that

$$F(\tau) = \left(\frac{f(X)}{\lambda + f(X)}\right)(1 - e^{-t(\lambda + f(X))})$$

$$\Rightarrow F'(\tau) = \frac{d}{dt}\left(\frac{f(X)}{\lambda + f(X)}\right)(1 - e^{-t(\lambda + f(X))})$$

$$= [\lambda + f(X)]e^{-t(\lambda + f(X))}\left(\frac{f(X)}{\lambda + f(X)}\right) = f(X)e^{-t(\lambda + f(X))}.$$

Therefore, the expectation of $\tau(X)$ is given as:

$$E\big[\tau(X)\big|\{\tau(X) \le (\tau(Y),\, t)\}\big]$$

$$= \int_0^\infty \left[tf(X)e^{-t(\lambda+f(X))}\right]dt = \int_0^\infty t\big(\lambda + f(X)\big)e^{-t(\lambda+f(X))}dt - \int_0^\infty \lambda te^{-t(\lambda+f(X))}dt\,.$$

$$\underbrace{\phantom{\int_0^\infty t\big(\lambda + f(X)\big)e^{-t(\lambda+f(X))}dt}}_{Q} \quad \underbrace{\phantom{\int_0^\infty \lambda te^{-t(\lambda+f(X))}dt}}_{R}$$

For part Q, let $v = t$ and $u = -e^{-t(\lambda+f(x))}$, so that $dv = dt$ and $du = (\lambda + f(X))e^{-t(\lambda+f(x))}dt$. Therefore,

$$\int_0^\infty t(\lambda + f)e^{-t(\lambda+f(X))}dt = \int v\,du = uv - \int u\,dv$$

$$= \left[-te^{-t(\lambda+f(X))}\right]_0^\infty + \int_0^\infty e^{-t(\lambda+f(X))}dt$$

$$= \left[-te^{-t(\lambda+f(X))}\right]_0^\infty + \left[-\frac{1}{(\lambda+f(X))}e^{-t(\lambda+f(X))}\right]^\infty$$

$$-\left[-\frac{1}{(\lambda+f)}e^{-t(y+f(X))}\right]^0$$

$$= 0 + 0 + \frac{1}{(\lambda+f(X))} = \frac{1}{(\lambda+f(X))}\,.\text{ For part R, let } v = t \text{ and}$$

$$u = -\frac{1}{(\lambda+f)}e^{-t(\lambda+f(X))},\text{ such that } v = dt \text{ and } du = e^{-t(\lambda+f(X))}dt.$$

Therefore,

$$\lambda\int_0^\infty e^{-t(\lambda+f(X))}dt = \lambda \int v\,du = \lambda uv - \lambda\int u\,dv$$

$$= \left[-\frac{\lambda t}{(\lambda+f(X))}e^{-t(\lambda+f(X))}\right]_0^\infty + \lambda\int_0^\infty \frac{e^{-t(\lambda+f(X))}}{(\lambda+f(X))}dt$$

$$= \left[-\frac{\lambda t}{(\lambda+f(X))}e^{-t(\lambda+f(X))}\right]_0^\infty + \left[-\frac{e^{-t(\lambda+f(X))}}{(\lambda+f(X))^2}\right]_0^\infty$$

$$= (0 - 0) + (-\lambda.0) + \frac{\lambda}{\left(\lambda + f(X)\right)^2} = \frac{\lambda}{\left(\lambda + f(X)\right)^2} \ .$$

$$\therefore \mathrm{E}(\tau) = \mathrm{Q} - \mathrm{R} = \frac{1}{\left(\lambda + f(X)\right)} - \frac{\lambda}{\left(\lambda + f(X)\right)^2} = \frac{f(X)}{\left[\lambda + f(X)\right]^2}$$

Bibliography

Amihud, Yakov and Maurizio Murgia, 1997, "Dividends, Taxes, and Signaling: Evidence from Germany," *Journal of Finance*, 397–408.

Arditti, D. Fred and John M. Pinkerton, 1978, "The valuation and Cost of Capital of the Levered Firm with Growth Opportunities," *Journal of Finance* 23:1 (March), 65–73.

Austin, H. David, 1993, "An Event-Study Approach to Measuring Innovative Output: The Case of Biotechnology," *American Economic Review* 83 (May), 253–258.

Baldwin, Y. Carliss, 1982, "Optimal Sequential Investment When Capital is Not Readily Reversible," *Journal of Finance* 37:3 (June), 763–782.

Barzel, Yoram, 1968, "Optimal Timing of Innovations," *Review of Economics and Statistics* (August), 348–355.

Bender, David and Bruno Leone (eds.), 1996, *Genetic Engineering: Opposing Viewpoints*. Greenhaven Press, San Diego.

Ben-Zion, Uri, 1984, "The R&D and Investment Decision and Its Relationship to the Firm's Market Value: Some Preliminary Results," in Zvi Griliches (Ed.), *R&D, Patents, and Productivity* (University of Chicago Press), 299–312.

Berk, B. Jonathan, Richard C. Green, and Vasant Naik, 1999, "Valuation and Return Dynamics of New Ventures," *Journal of Finance*, 1553–1607.

Bhattacharya, S., 1979, "Imperfect Information, Dividend Policy, and 'The Bird in the Hand' Fallacy," *Bell Journal of Economics*, Spring, 259–270.

Bjerksund, Peter and S. Ekern, 1990, "Managing Investment Opportunities Under Price Uncertainty: From 'Last Chance' to 'Wait and See' Strategies," *Financial Management*, Autumn, 65–83.

Black, Fischer and M. Scholes, 1973, "The Pricing of Options and Corporate Liabilities," *Journal of Political Economy* (May/June), 637–654.

145

Blose, E. Laurence and J.C.P. Shieh, 1997, "Tobin's q-Ratio and Market Reaction to Capital Investment Announcements," *Financial Review* 32:3, 449–476.

Bound, John, C. Cummins, Z. Griliches, B. Hall, and J. Adam, 1984, "Who does R&D and Who Patents?" in Zvi Griliches (Ed.), *R&D, Patents, and Productivity* (University of Chicago Press), 21–54.

Brealy, A. Richard and Stewart C. Myers, 1996, *Principal of Corporate Finance,* 5th Edition (New York: Irwin-McGraw-Hill).

Brennan, M., and E. Schwartz, 1985, "Evaluating Natural Resource Investments," *Journal of Business* 58:2 (April), 135–157.

Brown, Eryn, Mary J. Cronin, Ann Harrington, Jane Hodges, Justin Fox and Patricia Nakache, 1999, "9 Ways to Win on the Web," *Fortune* (May 24), 112–125.

Broyles, J.E. and I.A. Cooper, 1981, "Growth Opportunities and Real Investment Decisions," in Frans G.J. Derkinderen and Roy L. Crum (Eds.), *Risk, Capital Costs, and Project Financing Decisions* (Boston: Martinus Nijhoff Publishing), 107–118.

Bull, T. Allan, Geoffrey Holt and Malcolm D. Lilly, 1982, *Biotechnology: International Trends and Perspectives* (Paris: Organization for Economic Cooperation and Development.)

Burton, M. Burton, 1996, "Eli Lilly Wants to Reduce its Dependence on Prozac," *The Wall Street Journal,* June 12.

Carey, John, March 10, 1997, "DNA for Dummies: The Basics You Need to Know." *BusinessWeek,* 84–85.

Carey, John, Naomi Freundlich, Julie Flynn, and Neil Gross, March 10, 1997, "The Biotech Century." *BusinessWeek,* 78–90.

Carr, Peter, 1988, "The Valuation of Sequential Exchange Opportunities," *Journal of Finance* 43:5 (December), 1235–1256.

Chan, H. Su, J.D. Martin, and J.W. Kensinger, 1990, "Corporate Research and Development Expenditures and Share Value," *Journal Financial Economics* 26, 255–276.

Chung, K. H. and C. Charoenwong, 1991, "Investment Options, Assets in Place, and the Risk of Stocks," *Financial Management* (Autumn), 21–23.

Cockburn, Iaian and Z. Griliches, 1988, "Industry Effects and Appropriability Measures in the Stock Market's Valuation of R&D and Patents," *American Economic Review* 78 (May), 419–423.

Colvin, Geoffrey, 1999, "How to be a Great E-CEO," *Fortune* (May 24), 104–110.

Copeland, E. Thomas and J.F. Weston, 1988, *Financial Theory and Corporate Policy,* Third Edition (Addison-Wesley Publishing Company).

Cox, J.C., S.A. Ross and M. Rubinstein, 1979, "Option Pricing: A Simplified Approach," *Journal of Financial Economics*, 7, 229–263.

Dasgupta, Partha and J. Stiglitz, 1980, "Uncertainty, Industrial Structure, and the Speed of R&D," *Bell Journal of Economics* 11:1, 1–28.

Deng, Zhen, Baruch Lev, and Francis Narin, 1999, "Science and Technology as Predictors of Stock Performance." *Financial Analysts Journal*, 55:3 (May/June), 20–32.

Elmer-Dewitt, Philip, January 16, 1995, "Fat Times." *Time Magazine*, 58–65.

Fama, Eugene F., 1990, "Stock Returns, Expected Returns, and Real Activity," *Journal of Finance* 45, 1089–1109.

Fama, F. Eugene and K.R. French, 1992, "The Cross-section of expected Stock Returns," *Journal of Finance* 47, 427–465.

Fama, F. Eugene and K.R. French, 1997, "Taxes, Financing decisions, and Firm Value," *Working Paper W.P.440,* The University of Chicago Graduate School of Business.

Fama, Eugene F., and J.D. MacBeth, 1973, "Risk, Return, and Equilibrium: Empirical Tests," *Journal of Political Economy* 81, 607–636.

Fischer, Stanley, 1978, "Call Option Pricing When the Exercise Price is Uncertain, and the Valuation of Index Bonds," *Journal of Finance* 23:1 (March), 169–176.

Freundlich, Naomi, March 10, 1997, "Finding a Cure in DNA?" *Business-Week*, 90–92.

Gay, D. Gerald and Jouahn Nam, 1998, "The Under-investment Problem and Corporate Derivative Use," *Financial Management*, 27:4, 53–69.

Glen, Jack and Pinto, Brian, 1995, "Capital Markets and Developing Country Firms," *Finance & Development* (March), 40–43.

Gompers, A. Paul, 1995, "Optimal Investment, Monitoring, and the Staging of Venture Capital," *Journal of Finance*, 1461–1489.

Gordon, M.J., 1955, "The Pay-Off Period and the Rate of Profit," *Journal of Business* 28 (October), 253–260.

Gorman, Christine, January 16, 1995, "Desperately Seeking a Flab-Fighting Formula." *Time Magazine*, 62–63.

Graham, Benjamin and David L. Dodd, 1934, *Security Analysis.* New York: Whittlesey House, McGraw-Hill.

Griliches, Zvi, 1981, "Market Value, R&D, and Patents," *Economic Letters* 7:2, 183–187.

Hall, H. Bronwyn, 1993, "The Stock Market's Valuation of R&D Investment During the 1980's," *American Economic Review* 83 (May), 259–264.

Hamilton, O'C. Joan and Julie Flynn, March 10, 1997, "When Science Fiction Becomes Reality." *BusinessWeek*, 84–85.

Harris, Milton and A. Raviv, 1991, "The Theory of Capital Structure," *Journal of Finance*, 297–355.

Hayes and Garvin, 1982, "Managing as if Tomorrow Mattered," *Harvard Business Review* (May/June), 71–79.

Himelstein, Linda, Heather Green, Richard Siklos and Catherine Yang, 1998, "Yahoo! The Company, the Strategy, the Stock," *Business Week*, September 7, 66–76.

Hull, C. John, 1996, *Options, Futures, and Other Derivative Securities*, Third Edition (Englewood Cliffs, NJ: Prentice-Hall).

Hull, John and A. White, 1993, "Efficient Procedures for Valuing European and American Path-Dependent Options," *The Journal of Derivatives* (Fall), 21–31.

Ibbotson Associates, 1997, *Stocks, Bonds, Bills, and Inflation: 1997 Yearbook*, Chicago.

Ingersoll, Jr., E. Jonathan, 1987, *Theory of Financial Decision-Making* (Rowman & Littlefield Publishers, Inc.).

Jaffe, Adam, 1986, "Technological Opportunity and Spillovers of R&D: Evidence from Firm's Patents, Profits, and Market Value," *American Economic Review* 76, 984–1001.

Jensen, C. Michael, 1986, "Agency Costs of Free-Cash-Flow, Corporate Finance, and Takeovers," *American Economic Review* 76, 323–329.

Jensen, M., and W. Meckling, 1976, "Theory of the Firm: Managerial Behavior, Agency Costs, and Ownership Structure," *Journal of Financial Economics*, 305–360.

John, K. and J. Williams, 1985, "Dividends, Dilution and Taxes: A Signaling Equilibrium," *Journal of Finance*, 1053–1070.

Kamien, I. Morton and Schwartz, L. Nancy, 1980, "A Generalized Hazard Rate," *Economic Letters* 5, 245–249.

Kemna, G.Z. Angelien, 1993, "Case Studies on Real Options," *Financial Management*, Autumn, 259–270.

Kensinger, W. John, 1987, Adding the Value of Active Management into the Capital Budgeting Equation," *Midland Corporate Finance Journal* 5:1, 31–42.

Kester, W. Carl, 1984, "Today's Options for Tomorrow's Growth," *Harvard Business Review*, (March–April): 153–160.

Kester, W. Carl, 1986, "An Options Approach to Corporate Finance." Chapter 5 in *Handbook of Corporate Finance*, 2nd ed., Edited by E.I. Altman. New York, John Wiley & Sons.

Kester, W. Carl, 1993, "Turning Growth Options into Real Assets," in R. Aggarwal (Ed.), *Capital Budgeting Under Uncertainty* (Englewood Cliffs, NJ: Prentice-Hall), 187–207.

King, T. Ralph and Stephen D. Moore, November 29, 1995, "Basel's Drug Giants are Placing Huge Bets on U.S. Biotech Firms." *The Wall Street Journal*, A1 & A5.

Kothari, S.P. and J. Shanken, 1992, "Stock Return Variation and expected Dividends: A Time Series and Cross-sectional Analysis," *Journal of Financial Economics* 3, 305–360.

Langreth, Robert and Bruce Ingersoll, November 25, 1997, "FDA Approves New Diet Drug Made by Knoll." *The Wall Street Journal*, B1 & B10.

Langreth, Robert, December, 1997, "Merck Study Indicates Its Drug Provides Faster Relief for Migraine Headaches." *The Wall Street Journal*.

Lee, Tom and Wilde, L. Louis, 1980, "Market Structure and Innovation: A Reformulation," *Quarterly Journal of Economics* (March), 429–436.

Lindenberg, B. Eric and Ross A. Stephen, 1981, "Tobin's q Ratio and Industrial Organization," *Journal of Business* 54:1, 1–32.

Lintner, John, 1963, "The Cost of Capital and Optimal Financing of Corporate Growth," *Journal of Finance* 18, 292–310.

Long, S. Michael and Ileen B. Malitz, 1985, "Investment Patterns and Financial Leverage," in B.M. Friedman (Ed.), *Corporate Capital Structures in the United States* (The University of Chicago Press), 325–351.

Loury, C. Glenn, 1979, "Market Structure and Innovation," *Quarterly Journal of Economics* (August), 395–410.

Majd, Saman and R.S. Pindyck, 1987, "Time to Build, Option Value, and Investment Decisions," *Journal of Financial Economics*, 18:7–27.

Margrabe, William, 1978, "The value of an Option to Exchange one Asset for Another," *Journal of Finance* 23:1, 177–186.

Mason, S.P. and R.C. Merton, 1985, "The Role of Contingent Claims Analysis in Corporate Finance," in E.I. Altman and M Subrahmanyam (Eds.), *Recent Advances in Corporate Finance* (Homewood, IL: Richard D. Irwin), 7–54.

McConnell, J. John and C.J. Muscarella, 1985, "Corporate Capital Expenditure Decisions and the Market Value of the firm," *Journal of Financial Economics* 14, 399–422.

McDonald, L. Robert and D. Siegel, 1985, "Investment and the Valuation of Firms when there is an Option to Shut Down," *International Economic Review* 26:2, 331–349.

McDonald, L. Robert and D. Siegel, 1986, "The Value of Waiting to Invest," *The Quarterly Journal of Economics*, November, 707–727.

Megna, Pamela and M. Klock, 1993, "The Impact of Intangible Capital on Tobin's q in the Semiconductor Industry," *American Economic Review* 83 (May), 265–269.

Merton, R.C., 1974, "On the Pricing of Corporate Debt: The Risk Structure of Interest Rates," *Journal of Finance*, 19:2, 449–70.

Miller, M.H. and F. Modigliani, 1961, "Dividend Policy, Growth and the Valuation of Shares," *Journal of Business* 33 (October), 411–433.

Miller, M.H. and K. Rock, 1985, "Dividend Policy Under Asymmetric Information," *Journal of Finance*, 1031–1051.

Modigliani, F. and M.H. Miller, 1958, "The Cost of Capital, Corporation Finance and the Theory of Investment." *American Economic Review* 48 (June), 261–297.

Moore, D. Stephen, June 10, 1997, "Zeneca's Cancer Approach Catches On." *The Wall Street Journal*.

Moses, Vivian and Ronald E. Cape (eds.), 1994, *Biotechnology: The Science and the Business*. Harwood Academic Publishers, Switzerland.

Myers, C. Stewart, 1977, "Determinants of Corporate Borrowing," *Journal of Financial Economics* 5, 147–175.

Myers, C. Stewart, 1984, "The Capital Structure Puzzle," *Journal of Finance*, 575–592.

Myers, C. Stewart and N. Majluf, 1984, "Corporate Financing and Investment Decisions When Firms Have Information that Investors Do not Have," *Journal of Financial Economics*, 187–221.

Nocera, Joseph, 1999, "Do You Believe? How Yahoo! Became a Blue Chip," *Fortune* (June 7), 76–92.

Office of Technology Assessment, Congress of the United States, 1984, *Commercial Biotechnology: An International Analysis*, Pergamon Press, New York.

Ottoo, Richard, 1998, "Valuation of Internal Growth Opportunities: The Case of a Biotechnology Company." *The Quarterly Review of Economics and Finance*, 38 (Special Issue), 615–633.

Ottoo, Richard, 1998, "Growth Opportunities and Capital Structure of Emerging Firms: Theory and Empirical Evidence," Ph.D. Dissertation, The Zicklin School of Business, Baruch College, The City University of New York.

Paddock, L. James, D.R. Siegel and J.L. Smith, 1988, "Option Valuation of Claims on Real Assets: The Case of Offshore Petroleum Leases," *The Quarterly Journal of Economics* (August), 479–508.

Pennings, Enrico, and Onno Lint, 1997, "The Option Value of Advanced R&D," *European Journal of Operational Research*, 103, 83–94.

Pilotte, Eugene, 1992, "Growth Opportunities and the Stock Price Response to New Financing," *Journal of Business* 65:3, 371–393.

Pindyck, S. Robert, 1988, "Irreversible Investment, Capacity Choice, and the Value of the Firm." *The American Economic Review* 78:5 (December), 969–985.

Pindyck, S. Robert, 1993, "Investments of Uncertain Costs," *Journal of Financial Economics* 34, 53–76.

Posner, M.J.M, and D. Zuckerman, 1990, "Optimal R&D Programs in a Random Environment," *Journal of Applied Probability,* 27, 343–350.

Roberts, Kevin and Martin L. Weitzman, 1981, "Funding Criteria for Research, Development, and Exploration Projects," *Econometrica* 49, 1261–1288.

Ross, Sheldon, 1994, *A First Course in Probability,* Fourth Edition. Macmillan College Publishing Company, Inc., New York.

Ross, S.A., 1977, "The Determination of Financial Structure: Incentive-Signaling Approach," *Bell Journal of Economics,* Spring, 23–40.

Schmitt, W. Roland, 1985, "Successful Corporate R&D," *Harvard Business Review* (May–June), 124–128.

Schlender, Brent, 1999, "Larry Ellison: Oracle at Web Speed," *Fortune* (May 24), 128–136.

Schumpeter, Joseph, 1942, *Capitalism, Socialism, and Democracy.* (New York: Harper and Row).

Schwartz, D. Nelson, 1999, "Web Bets 9 Ways to Ride the Net," *Fortune* (June 7), 95–100.

Shevlin, Terry, 1991, "The Valuation of R&D Firms with R&D Limited Partnerships," *The Accounting Review* 66:1, 1–21.

Stulz, M. Rene, 1990, "Managerial Discretion and Optimal Financing Policies," *Journal of Financial Economics* 26, 3–27.

Szewczyk, H. Samuel, George P. Tsetsekos, and Zaher Zantout, 1996, "The Valuation of Corporate R&D Expenditures: Evidence from Investment Opportunities and Free Cash Flow," *Financial Management* 25:1(Spring), 105–110.

Tanouye, Elyse, November 24, 1995, "SmithKline Leads in Race to Use Genetics to Find Drugs." *The Wall Street Journal,* A1 & A5.

Thakor, V. Anjan, Hong and S. Greenbaum, 1981, "Bank Loan Commitments and Interest Rate Volatility," *Journal of Banking and Finance,* 5, 497–510.

Thomadakis, B. Stavros, 1976, "A Model of Market Power, Valuation and the Firm's Returns," *Bell Journal of Economics* 17:1, 150–162.

Thomadakis, B. Stavros, 1977, "A Value-Based Test of Profitability and Market Structure," *The Review of Economics and Statistics* 59, 179–185.

Trester, J. Jeffrey, 1993, "Venture Capital Contracting Under Asymmetric Information." *Working Paper,* The Wharton Financial Institutions

Center (The Wharton School of the University of Pennsylvania).

Trigeorgis, Lenos, 1993, "Real options and Interactions with Financial Flexibility," *Financial Management* (Autumn), 202–224.

Trigeorgis, Lenos, 1990, "A Real-Options Application in Natural Resource Investments," *Advances in Futures and Options Research,* 4, 153–164.

Trigeorgis, Lenos, 1988, "A Conceptual Options Framework for Capital Budgeting," *Advances in Futures and options Research,* 3, 145–167.

Trigeorgis, Lenos and S.P. Mason, 1987, "Valuing Managerial Flexibility," *Midland Corporate Finance Journal* 5:1 (Spring), 14–21.

Waldholz, Michael, June 18, 1997, "Glaxo Picks Allen Roses, Trailblazer in Alzheimer's, to Head Genetics Unit." *The Wall Street Journal,* B8.

Weber, Joseph, December 2, 1991, "This Pill Could Reduce the Chance of a Heart Attack." *BusinessWeek,* 39.

Weber, Joseph, John Byrne, Mike McNamee, and Gary McWilliams, June 27, 1994, "Merck Finally Gets its Man." *BusinessWeek,* 22–25.

Weitzman, Martin, Whitney Newey, and Michael Rabin, 1981, "Sequential R&D Strategy for Synfuels," Bell *Journal of Economics* 12, 574–590.

Willner, Ram, 1995, "Valuing Start-up Venture Growth Options," in Lenos Trigeorgis (Ed.), *Real Options in Capital Investment: Models, Strategies, and Applications* (Westport, CT: Praeger Publisher).

Author Index

Stulz, Rene, 19, 93, 133, 134
Szewczyk, Samuel, 129n, 134

T
Thakor, V., 90
Thomadakis, Stavros, 129n
Trigeorgis, Lenos, 23, 25, 73, 90
Trueman, B., 25n
Tsetsekos, George, 129n, 134

W
Weitzman, Martin, 43n
Williams, J., 24n
Wilde, Louis, 42n

Z
Zantout, Zaher, 129n

Subject Index